CROCKPOT SLOW COOKER COOKBOOK 2024

1001 DAYS FRESH AND DELICIOUS CROCK POT SLOW COOKER RECIPES FOR BEGINNERS & ADVANCED USERSAND PROS

Hayden Thomson

First paperback edition May 2023.
Cover art by Natalie M. Kern
Printed by Amazon in the USA.

Disclaimer : Although the author and publisher have made every effort to ensure that the information in this book was correct at press time, the author and publisher do not assume and hereby disclaim any liability to any party for any loss, damage, or disruption caused by errors or omissions, whether such errors or omissions result from negligence, accident, or any other cause. this book is not intended as a substitute for the medical advice of physicians.

CONTENTS

MEAT RECIPES 64

OTHER FAVORITE RECIPES 88

FISH AND SEAFOOD RECIPES 95

DESSERT RECIPES 100

INTRODUCTION

How does my slow cooker work? At what temperature does my slow cooker cook? How do I convert my favorite recipe to the slow cooker? How much energy does my slow cooker use? These are just a few of the many questions our experts manning the phones receive regularly about slow cooking. This post will tell you what a slow cooker is, how it works and what you can do with it to make cooking at home simple, convenient and delicious.

WHAT IS A SLOW COOKER?

A slow cooker allows unattended home cooking for long periods of time at relatively low cooking temperatures. It's made up of three main components: the base (this contains the heating element which is attached to a liner), the vessel and the lid. The base of the slow cooker is the part you see the most. It has handles, a temperature knob or control panel, and feet that keep it slightly raised off the surface of your counter. The liner is a thin metal insert melded onto the inside of the slow cooker base. You can't see or access the electrical workings between the liner and the base, but this houses heater bands that conduct heat around the bottom of the slow cooker. The bands create heat that transfers to the cooking vessel and rises across the the bottom and up the sides, uniformly cooking your food. There is a small gap between the liner and the outer wrap of the base for airflow, which keeps the outside from overheating.

The cooking vessel is where you put the food you cook. It's usually made from heavy stoneware, which helps keep the heat constant, stabilized and evenly distributed. Some slow cookers have clips to hold the lid in place for easy, no-spill traveling. The lid is important because you can't reach the appropriate cooking temperatures without it. Imagine trying to bring pasta water to a boil with a lid and then without it. The lid to your slow cooker works the same way.

Some slow cookers have steam vent holes in their lids; the Set & Forget® Programmable Slow Cooker has a probe hole. If you're not inserting the probe for use in PROBE mode, leave the hole open and don't plug it up. Vent holes allow steam to escape and the wattage of the unit has been adjusted to compensate for any heat loss.

HOW DOES MY SLOW COOKER WORK?

Cooking with a slow cooker is most similar to cooking with a Dutch oven on a stovetop. On a stovetop, a pot is heated from the bottom and the heat rises up the sides of the pot to heat the food within. Similarly, a slow cooker creates heat toward the base, which transfers up the sides of the vessel to heat the food within. In addition, setting the temperature for both cooking methods is very similar. Instead of cooking something at a specific temperature on the stovetop, you set the temperature to low or high. Your slow cooker works in the same manner.

When you set the temperature to low on your slow cooker, your heating element will put out less heat. When you set the temperature to high, the heating element will put out more heat. Cooking something on low takes more time than cooking something on high. Because the temperature settings work most like stovetop cooking, it is hard to give an actual temperature for the various heat levels.

HOW DO I CONVERT A STOVETOP OR OVEN RECIPE TO THE SLOW COOKER?

Slow cooking is relatively forgiving and is adaptable to a wide variety of recipes. Slow cookers use low cooking temperatures and retain moisture during the cooking process. If your recipe calls for using the oven to dry food, it probably won't work in the slow cooker. Likewise, if your recipe calls for very high temperatures of oil to fry things quickly, a slow cooker will not be an option. However, if your recipe calls for cooking something "low and slow," the slow cooker will work excellently.

Many recipes for sauces and dips call for cooking on the slow cooker's HIGH setting or for only 1-2 hours. Long cooking times of 6-7+ hours or using the LOW setting is best for roasts and large or tough cuts of meat, like a pulled pork shoulder. The majority of slow cooker-friendly recipes can be adapted to cook somewhere in the middle; stews and soups fall into this category.

You can convert your favorite recipes to slow cooker recipes if you learn these important differences first:
- Liquids do not evaporate in a slow cooker. Unless you are cooking rice, pasta, or beans, reduce the amount of liquid to about half the amount called for in your recipe.

- Fresh vegetables produce the most desirable results. Potatoes, carrots, onions and garlic should be washed and cut in uniform pieces, then placed in the bottom of the crock. Canned and frozen vegetables take less time to cook and can result in overcooked dishes.

- Ground beef should be browned and drained before slow cooking to remove grease.

- Tender foods such as pasta, squash, asparagus or peas should be added in the last hour of cooking.

- Seafood such as shrimp, scallops and fish should be added in the last 15-30 minutes of cooking.

- Dairy products such as cheese, milk and sour cream should be added at the end of cooking.

IS MY SLOW COOKER ENERGY EFFICIENT?

We like to say slow cooking is energy efficient for you AND your home. Slow cooking gives you the ability to cook while you are away, saving you time and energy. It's great to have a home-cooked meal ready for your family when you arrive home from work, isn't it?

The slow cooker is not just efficient for you, it's efficient for your home. A small slow cooker uses approximately the same power as one and a half 100 watt light bulbs. Because it cooks with contained heat, it uses less energy. And since it's an appliance that's intended to be used unattended, there's no need to worry about it while you're gone.

Crock-Pot is the name of a brand that first came on the market in the 1970s. It has a stoneware pot that is surrounded by a heating element, whereas a slow cooker is typically a metal pot that sits on top of a heated surface. The term slow cooker is not a brand but rather refers to the type of appliance.

The Tower Slow Cooker feels robust and reliable, and even when filled with hot stew or curry, lifting was easy and not too heavy. The outer casing did get a little hot when cooking on high, and we felt it preferable to stand the cooker on a heatproof mat to prevent any worktop damage.

BREAKFAST AND BRUNCH RECIPES

Easy Slow-cooker Lasagne

🍽 Servings: 6   🕐 Cooking Time: 4 Hours And 25 Mins.

Ingredients:

- 1 tbsp extra virgin olive oil
- 1kg veal mince
- 90g (1/3 cup) tomato paste
- 125ml (1/2 cup) red wine
- 680g Coles Mum's Sause Bolognese
- 250ml (1 cup) Massel chicken style liquid stock
- 1 tbsp dried oregano leaves
- 250g pkt dried lasagne sheets
- 600ml ctn pouring cream
- 3 eggs, lightly whisked
- 300g (3 cups) coarsely grated three cheese mix
- Fresh curly parsley leaves, to serve

Directions:

1. Heat the oil in a large frying pan over high heat. Cook the mince, stirring with a wooden spoon to break up any lumps, for 10 minutes or until the mince changes colour. Add the tomato paste. Cook, stirring, for 1 minute to coat. Add the wine. Cook for 1 minute or until the wine evaporates. Add the pasta sauce, stock and oregano. Season. Simmer for 10 minutes or until reduced slightly.

2. Meanwhile, whisk the cream and eggs in a bowl until well combined. Season. Stir in 2 cups cheese.

3. Grease the insert of a 5L slow cooker. Spread a thin layer of the mince mixture over the base of the insert. Cover with a layer of lasagne sheets, breaking the sheets to fit, if necessary. Drizzle one-fifth of the cream mixture over the lasagne sheets and top with one-quarter of the remaining mince mixture. Continue layering with remaining lasagne sheets, cream mixture and mince mixture, finishing with a layer of cream mixture. Sprinkle with remaining 1 cup cheese.

4. Cook on Low for 3 1/2 - 4 hours or until the lasagne sheets are tender and the liquid is mostly absorbed. Carefully remove the insert from the slow cooker. Set aside, covered, for 10-15 minutes to rest. Sprinkle with parsley.

5. RECIPE NOTES

6. The lasagne sheets can be broken up into smaller pieces to fit into the slow cooker. It doesn't matter if the pieces overlap.

Black Bean Burritos Recipe

👥 Servings: 6   🕐 Cooking Time: 3 Hours

Ingredients:

- For the black bean filling
- 450g (14 1/2oz) dry black turtle beans
- 1 tbsp olive oil
- 1 onion, finely chopped
- 2 garlic cloves, crushed
- 1 tsp ground cumin
- 2 spring onions finely diced
- 1 tsp smoked paprika
- 1 tsp chilli powder
- For the Pico de gallo
- 6 ripe tomatoes, deseeded and diced
- 1 onion, finely diced
- 1/2 red chilli, very finely chopped
- 1 garlic clove, crushed
- 1/2 reserved coriander leaves, chopped
- 1 lime, juiced
- For the guacamole
- 4 ripe cherry or baby plum tomatoes, finely chopped
- 3 avocados, very ripe
- 1/2 red onion, finely diced
- 1 red chilli, finely diced
- small bunch of coriander, stems finely chopped (reserve leaves for later)
- 1 large lime, juiced
- To serve
- 12-18 large flour tortillas
- 150g mature Cheddar, grated
- 1/2 reserved coriander leaves

Directions:

1. Soak the black beans in cold water to soften for 24 hours.

2. The next day, drain the beans well, heat the olive oil in a large saucepan and fry the onion, garlic and cumin for 5 minutes until they start to colour. Add the beans and mix well. Pour over boiling water until the bean mixture is covered about 7cm (3ins), of liquid put on the lid and simmer for 2 hours.

3. While the beans are cooking, mix together all the pico de gallo ingredients apart from the coriander. Add 1 tsp sea salt and mix well. Cover and leave at room temperature.

4. When the beans are cooked and soft, drain well. In a very large frying pan, add the remaining oil and fry the onion, garlic, spring onion and spices until golden, then add the beans. Using a potato masher, partially mash the beans and mix well while cooking for 15 minutes.

5. Meanwhile, make the guacamole. Roughly mash the avocados and lime in a bowl. Mix in the other ingredients and cover with cling film.

6. Add the remaining coriander to the pico de gallo and grate the cheese. Microwave the tortillas for 10 seconds to soften. To serve, take one tortilla, top with beans, pico de gallo, guacamole, cheese and coriander and roll up the tortilla. Repeat until everything is used up.

Yummy Golden Syrup Flapjacks

 Servings: 12   🕐 Cooking Time: 15 Mins.

Ingredients:

- 250g jumbo porridge oats
- 125g butter, plus extra for the tin
- 125g light brown sugar
- 2-3 tbsp golden syrup (depending on how gooey you want it)

Directions:

1. Heat the oven to 200C/180C fan/gas 6. Put the oats, butter, sugar and golden syrup in a food processor and pulse until mixed – be careful not to overmix or the oats may lose their texture.

2. Lightly butter a 20 x 20cm baking tin and add the mixture. Press into the corners with the back of a spoon so the mixture is flat and score into 12 squares. Bake for around 15 mins until golden brown.

Slow-cooked Coconut Porridge With Warm Tropical Fruit Recipe

👥 Servings: 4

Ingredients:

- 100g jumbo rolled oats
- ¼ tsp cinnamon
- 400ml tin coconut milk
- clear honey, to sweeten (optional)
- 1 tsp coconut oil
- 1 x 220g pack Mango & Pineapple with a Coconut & Lemongrass Drizzle

Directions:

1. Before you go to bed, put the oats in the slow cooker with the cinnamon and cover with the coconut milk. Fill the coconut tin with water and add that to the slow cooker. Cook on low for 6-7 hours, until the oats are soft and creamy. (If you prefer to cook this during the day, then give the oats a stir every now and then, but if you're doing it overnight don't worry.)

2. At the end of the cooking time, give the oats a good stir and add honey to sweeten if you like. Keep the oats warm while you prepare the pineapple and mango.

3. To serve one, heat the coconut oil in a frying pan and fry the fruits, tossing now and then, for 4-5 minutes until slightly softened and beginning to caramelise. Leave to cool slightly. Serve the porridge with the fruit, any juices from the pan and the drizzle if liked.

4. Serve with: Vanilla-spiced latte (this makes one)

5. Put 200g caster sugar in a small pan with 200ml water, 1 vanilla pod, halved lengthways and the seeds scraped out and mixed in, 6 green cardamom pods, split and the seeds ground and mixed in, and 1 cinnamon stick, broken.

6. Heat gently until the sugar has dissolved, then bring to the boil and bubble gently for 5 mins. Leave to cool in the pan overnight, for the flavours to infuse, then strain into a lidded jar.

7. This will keep for about a month in the fridge. To make one latte put 2-3 tbsp of the vanilla-spiced syrup into a mug and top with 50ml steaming hot espresso coffee and 150ml hot milk.

Chicken Pasta Bake

 Servings: 6   Cooking Time: 45 Mins.

Ingredients:

- 4 tbsp olive oil
- 1 onion, finely chopped
- 2 garlic cloves, crushed
- ¼ tsp chilli flakes
- 2 x 400g cans chopped tomatoes
- 1 tsp caster sugar

- 6 tbsp mascarpone
- 4 skinless chicken breasts, sliced into strips
- 300g penne
- 70g mature cheddar, grated
- 50g grated mozzarella
- ½ small bunch of parsley, finely chopped

Directions:

1. Heat 2 tbsp of the oil in a pan over a medium heat and fry the onion gently for 10-12 mins. Add the garlic and chilli flakes and cook for 1 min. Tip in the tomatoes and sugar and season to taste. Simmer uncovered for 20 mins or until thickened, then stir through the mascarpone.
2. Heat 1 tbsp of oil in a non-stick frying pan. Season the chicken and fry for 5-7 mins or until the chicken is cooked through.
3. Heat the oven to 220C/200C fan/gas 7. Cook the penne following pack instructions. Drain and toss with the remaining oil. Tip the pasta into a medium sized ovenproof dish. Stir in the chicken and pour over the sauce. Top with the cheddar, mozzarella and parsley. Bake for 20 mins or until golden brown and bubbling.

Prosciutto-pesto Breakfast Strata

 Servings: 10   Cooking Time: 50 Mins.

Ingredients:

- 2 cups 2% milk
- 1 cup white wine or chicken broth
- 1 loaf (1 pound) French bread, cut into 1/2-inch slice
- 1/4 cup minced fresh basil
- 1/4 cup minced fresh parsley
- 3 tablespoons olive oil
- 1/2 pound thinly sliced smoked Gouda cheese

- 1/2 pound thinly sliced prosciutto
- 3 medium tomatoes, thinly sliced
- 1/2 cup prepared pesto
- 4 large eggs
- 1/2 cup heavy whipping cream
- 1/2 teaspoon salt
- 1/4 teaspoon pepper

Directions:

1. In a shallow bowl, combine milk and wine. Dip both sides of bread in milk mixture; squeeze gently to remove excess liquid. Layer bread slices in a greased 13x9-in. baking dish.
2. Sprinkle with basil and parsley; drizzle with oil. Layer with half of the cheese, half of the prosciutto and all of the tomatoes; drizzle with half of the pesto. Top with remaining cheese, prosciutto and pesto.
3. In a small bowl, whisk eggs, cream, salt and pepper until blended; pour over top. Refrigerate, covered, several hours or overnight.
4. Preheat oven to 350°. Remove strata from refrigerator while oven heats. Bake, uncovered, until top is golden brown and a knife inserted in the center comes out clean, 50-60 minutes. Let stand 5-10 minutes before serving.

Slow Cooker Southwestern Cheesy Chicken Pasta

 Servings: 8   Cooking Time: 8 Hours.

Ingredients:

- 20 oz. Ro-tel (2 cans)
- 11 oz. can Mexicorn (or a can of southwestern corn mix), drained
- 3.8 oz. can olives, drained
- 1 tsp. chili powder
- 1/2 tsp. oregano
- 1/2 tsp. salt
- 1/4 tsp. pepper
- 1/4 tsp. cumin

- 2 lbs. boneless skin-less chicken breasts
- 2 cups shredded sharp cheddar cheese
- 16 oz. sour cream
- 1 lb. medium-sized shell pasta, cooked according to package directions, drained
- For Serving
- Additional shredded cheese
- Sliced green onions

Directions:

1. Add the Rotel, Mexicorn, olives, chili powder, oregano, salt, pepper and cumin to a 6-quart slow cooker, stir. Add the chicken into this mixture.
2. Cover and cook on LOW for 8 hours.
3. Shred the chicken with 2 forks right in the slow cooker.
4. Stir in the cheese and sour cream, then stir in the cooked and drained pasta.
5. Serve each serving with a sprinkle of more cheese, and then a sprinkle of green onion.

Notes:

1. How can I make this less spicy?
2. Use Mild Rotel if you can find it.
3. If you can't find mild Rotel, use 2 small jars of mild salsa.

Two-minute Breakfast Smoothie

 Servings: 2

Ingredients:

- 1 banana
- 1 tbsp porridge oats
- 80g soft fruit (whatever you have – strawberries, blueberries, and mango all work well)

- 150ml milk
- 1 tsp honey
- 1 tsp vanilla extract

Directions:

1. Put all the ingredients in a blender and whizz for 1 min until smooth.
2. Pour the banana oat smoothie into two glasses to serve.
3. RECIPE TIPS
4. MAKE THREE-MINUTE PANCAKES
5. Don't wash the blender – use it to make our three-minute banana pancakes as well.

Slow Cooker Pickled Pulled Pork Sandwiches

Servings: 9   **Cooking Time: 7 Hours**

Ingredients:

- 1 (5-6 lb.) boneless pork shoulder
- 1 (20 ounce) jar pepperoncini's with juices
- 1 (16 ounce) jar pickled okra with juices
- 1 (16 ounce) jar pickled mixed vegetables with juices
- 1 (8 ounce) jar pickled banana peppers with juices
- 1 cup pickled jalapenos, optional
- 12 ounces beer/lager of choice
- ½ yellow onion, thinly sliced
- 3 garlic cloves, roughly chopped
- 3 sprigs fresh thyme
- salt and pepper to taste
- 14 to 18 slices thick cut white bread, lightly toasted
- ☐ cup mayonnaise, divided

Directions:

1. Generously season pork shoulder with salt and pepper then place into a slow cooker.
2. Pour pickled ingredients into slow cooker followed by beer and top with onions, garlic and thyme. Add another dash of salt and pepper and place lid over contents.
3. Set slow cooker to high and cook for 6 to 7 hours, until shoulder is soft and easily falling apart.
4. Transfer pork shoulder into a large dish and scoop vegetables over the meat.
5. Using two forks, shred meat and vegetables together until completely shredded.
6. Spread each slice of toasted bread with some mayonnaise and top half of the slices with a heaping cup of pickled pulled pork. Top each pile of pulled pork with the remaining pieces of toasted bread, gently pressing down. Serve immediately.

Slow-cooker Irish Oats

Servings: 8-10

Ingredients:

- 4 cups frozen peach slices
- 2 cups steel-cut oats
- 2/3 cup packed brown sugar
- 1 tablespoon vanilla extract
- 1 teaspoon kosher salt
- 1 cup sliced almonds
- 1 cup flaked coconut
- 2 cups golden raisins
- 1 cup whole milk
- 1/4 cup heavy cream
- 1 cup fresh blueberries
- Honey, for drizzling

Directions:

1. Place the frozen peaches, oats, brown sugar, vanilla, salt and 8 cups water in the bowl of a slow cooker. Stir, set to low and cook for 6 to 8 hours or up to overnight.
2. Meanwhile, toast the sliced almonds and flaked coconut separately in dry nonstick skillets over medium heat, shaking the pans frequently to ensure an even toast, until golden and fragrant, 3 to 4 minutes. Let cool. Store, covered, until serving.
3. To serve, stir the raisins, milk and cream into the oat mixture. Spoon into bowls and garnish with the almonds, coconut, blueberries and a drizzle of honey.

SOUPS AND STEWS RECIPES

Slow Cooker Tuscan White Bean Soup

👥 Servings: 6   🕐 Cooking Time: 8 Hours

Ingredients:

- 30 oz. white beans, drained and rinsed (two 15-oz. cans)
- 30 oz. fire-roasted diced tomatoes (do not drain) (two 15-oz. cans)
- 2 cups sliced carrots
- 1 ½ cups diced celery
- 1 small white onion diced
- 1 garlic clove minced
- 2 bay leaves
- 1 tsp. dried oregano
- 1 tsp. dried thyme
- 1 tsp. dried rosemary
- 1 tsp. salt
- ¼ tsp. pepper
- 32 oz. box chicken broth
- 1 ½ lbs. boneless skinless chicken breasts
- For serving
- parmesan cheese
- bread

Directions:

1. Cooking instructions:
2. Add everything to the slow cooker. Cover and cook on LOW for 8 hours. Discard bay leaves. Shred the chicken with two forks right in the slow cooker. Serve topped with parmesan cheese. Enjoy!
3. To make this into a freezer meal:
4. Place everything into a gallon-sized Ziplock bag (before cooking), squeeze out air before sealing. Freeze for up to a month. Thaw in fridge for 36 hours, then follow cooking directions above.

Notes:

1. Storing instructions: Add any remaining soup to an airtight container and store it in the fridge for up to one week. It also freezes well (for up to 3 months).
2. Instead of chicken, cooked ground sausage, beef or turkey can be used.

Slow-cooker Chicken-tortilla Soup

Servings: 4   **Cooking Time:** Mins.

Ingredients:

- 1 1/4 lb. skinless, bone-in chicken thighs
- 1 small onion, chopped
- 1/2 red bell pepper, chopped
- 1 garlic clove, chopped
- 2 c. chicken stock
- 1 (14.5-oz.) can diced tomatoes, drained
- 1 (8-oz.) can tomato sauce
- 1 (4-oz.) can chopped green chiles
- 1 tsp. chili powder
- 1 tsp. dried oregano
- 3/4 tsp. ground cumin
- Kosher salt
- Freshly ground black pepper
- 2 yellow squash, halved and sliced
- 3 oz. green beans, halved
- 1 tbsp. fresh lime juice
- 2 1/2 tbsp. chopped fresh cilantro, plus more for serving
- Sliced jalapeños, sour cream, and tortilla chips, for serving

Directions:

1. Combine chicken, onion, bell pepper, garlic, stock, diced tomatoes, tomato sauce, chiles, chili powder, oregano, and cumin in a 4-quart slow cooker. Season with salt and pepper.
2. Cook, covered, until chicken is cooked through on low 7 to 8 hours or on high 3 to 4 hours. Add squash and green beans and cook, covered, for 30 minutes. Remove chicken, discard bones and shred meat; return to slow cooker. Stir in lime juice and cilantro.
3. Serve topped with cilantro, jalapeños, and sour cream, with tortilla chips alongside.

Slow Cooker Vegetarian Stew Recipe

👪 Servings: 4   🕑 Cooking Time: 4 Hours.

Ingredients:

- 1 onion, peeled and chopped
- 360g butternut squash, chopped into chunks
- 250g sweet mini peppers, seeded and halved
- 400g tin cannellini beans, drained and rinsed
- 400g tin chickpeas, drained and rinsed
- 400g tin chopped tomatoes
- 10-12 basil leaves, shredded
- 75g pine nuts, toasted
- 2 tbsp extra-virgin olive oil
- vegetarian hard cheese or Parmesan, shaved, to serve (optional)

Directions:

1. Put the onion, butternut squash, peppers, beans and chickpeas in the dish a slow cooker.
2. Pour over the chopped tomatoes then sprinkle with half the basil and season well. Stir well then set the slow cooker to low and cook for 4 hrs, until the vegetables are soft and tender.
3. Serve sprinkled with the remaining basil, the toasted pine nuts, a drizzle of olive oil and shavings of hard cheese, if you like.
4. Tip: Cooking pulses for a long time helps to make them more digestible and gives them a lovely creaminess – in this dish, any combination of beans or pulses would also work well.
5. Freezing
6. Once the cooked dish has cooled completely, transfer it to an airtight, freezer-safe container, seal and freeze for up to 1 month. To serve, defrost overnight before reheating thoroughly.

Slow-cooker Beef Bourguignon Soup

👪 Servings: 4   🕑 Cooking Time: 6 Hours 15 Mins.

Ingredients:

- 1 tbsp extra virgin olive oil
- 1 brown onion, diced
- 1 garlic clove, finely chopped
- 700g beef chuck steak, trimmed, cut into 2cm pieces
- 1/4 cup tomato paste
- 1 cup red wine
- 1 litre Massel beef style liquid stock
- 2 carrots, diced
- 1 celery stalk, trimmed, sliced
- 1 sprig fresh flat-leaf parsley
- 2 sprigs fresh thyme
- 200g button mushrooms, thickly sliced
- Fresh flat-leaf parsley, extra, to serve
- 4 slices crusty bread, to serve

Directions:

1. Heat 1/2 the oil in a large non-stick frying pan over medium-high heat. Add onion and garlic. Cook, stirring often, for 5 minutes or until softened. Transfer to the bowl of a 5.5-litre slow cooker.
2. Heat remaining oil in pan over mediumhigh heat. Add beef. Cook for 5 minutes or until browned. Add tomato paste. Cook, stirring, for 1 minute. Add wine. Bring to a simmer. Simmer for 2 minutes. Transfer to slow cooker.
3. Add stock, carrot, celery, parsley and thyme to slow cooker. Cover. Cook on low for 6 hours (or high for 4 hours), adding mushrooms in the last 30 minutes of cooking time. Remove and discard parsley and thyme sprigs. Season with salt and pepper. Sprinkle with parsley and serve with crusty bread.

Slow Cooker Fish Stew Recipe

Servings: 6   **Cooking Time: 2 Hours**

Ingredients:

- 1 tsp. rapeseed oil
- 1 onion, sliced
- 2 roasted red peppers, from a jar, roughly diced
- 3 garlic cloves, finely sliced
- 1 tsp. grated fresh root ginger
- 1 tsp. sweet smoked paprika
- 1/4 tsp cayenne pepper
- 200 ml (7 fl oz (⅓ pint)) white wine
- 2 x 400 g tins chopped tomatoes

- 1/2 tsp caster sugar
- 2 fresh bay leaves
- Pinch saffron
- 500 g (1lb 2oz) clams
- 375 g (13oz) cod loin, cut into 3cm pieces
- 350 g (12oz) raw tiger prawns
- Juice 1 lime, plus extra wedges, to serve
- Small handful parsley leaves
- Crusty bread, to serve

Directions:

1. Heat the oil in a large casserole, add the onion and cook for 10min, until softened. Add the peppers, garlic, ginger and spices and cook for a further 3min. Pour in the wine and boil for 5min.

2. Tip in the tomatoes, sugar, bay leaves and saffron, bring to a simmer. Season, cover and cook for 1hr 30min. Remove from the heat, discard the bay leaves and, using a stick blender, whizz until smooth.

3. Return to the heat and bring to the boil. Add the clams, cover and cook for 5min. Reduce to a gentle simmer and add the cod, prawns and juice of 1 lime, continue cooking for 5min until the fish is just cooked through and the clams are open (discarding any unopened). Season to taste.

4. To serve, cut the remaining lime into wedges, divide the soup among 6 bowls, sprinkle with the parsley.

Notes:

1. Before adding the clams, rinse, tap and discard any that don't close or have damaged shells.

2. In a slow cooker: Prepare the vegetables as in step 1. Add the tomatoes, sugar, bay and saffron, bring to the boil and transfer to the dish of a slow cooker, set to low and leave for 4-6hr. Using a stick blender, whizz until smooth. Bring to the boil, add the clams and cook for 5min. Add the cod, prawns and juice of 1 lime. Continue as per recipe, until fish is cooked through.

3. Get ahead: Complete to end of step 3 up to 2 days in advance. Keep in an airtight container in the fridge. Complete recipe to serve.

Slow Cooker Chicken Gnocchi Soup

👪 Servings: 8-10   🕐 Cooking Time: 8 Hours

Ingredients:

- 1 lb. boneless skinless chicken breasts
- 2 cups mirepoix (just a simple mixture of chopped onions, celery, and carrots)
- 1–2 teaspoons dried basil
- 1–2 teaspoon Italian seasoning
- 1 teaspoon poultry seasoning
- 1 teaspoon salt
- 4 cups chicken broth
- 3 tablespoons cornstarch dissolved in 2 tablespoons water
- two 12 ounce cans evaporated milk
- two 1 lb. packages gnocchi (about 4 cups)
- 6 slices bacon
- 2–3 cloves garlic, minced
- 2 cups fresh baby spinach

Directions:

1. Place the chicken, mirepoix, basil, Italian seasoning, poultry seasoning, salt, and broth in a Slow Cooker or slow cooker. Cover and cook on high for 4-5 hours or low for 6-8 hours. Shred the chicken directly in the crockpot.

2. Add the cornstarch mixture, evaporated milk, and gnocchi. Stir and replace cover. Cook another 45 minutes – 1 hour until the soup has thickened and the gnocchi has softened.

3. While the soup is thickening, cut the bacon into small pieces and fry until crispy. Drain on paper towels and wipe most of the bacon grease out of the pan, leaving just a little bit for the spinach/garlic. Add the garlic and saute for one minute. Add the spinach and stir until wilted. Remove from heat. Add the bacon and spinach to the crockpot. Stir to combine.

4. Add any additional liquid as needed (I added about a cup of water once it started to thicken) and season again with salt and pepper as needed.

Notes:

1. Be sure to taste and adjust with salt/pepper before serving. It may need more depending on the saltiness of your broth.

2. Instant Pot Instructions: Add the chicken, mirepoix, basil, Italian seasoning, poultry seasoning, salt, and broth to the Instant Pot. Cook for 20 minutes on high pressure. Let out the steam using quick release. Remove the chicken to shred, and then add it back to the pot. Stir in the cornstarch mixture, evaporated milk, and gnocchi. Then, use the "Saute" function to simmer the soup for another 20 minutes or so to thicken it all up. Add in the bacon and spinach, and stir to combine.

Beef And Ale Stew With Cheesy Croutons Recipe

Servings: 6   **Cooking Time: 2 Hours 30 Mins.**

Ingredients:

- 900g stewing steak, cut into matchbox-size pieces
- 3 tbsp plain flour, seasoned
- 2 tbsp olive oil
- 330ml bottle dark Belgian beer
- 25g butter
- 4 large onions, thickly sliced
- 2 sticks celery, thinly sliced
- 2 sticks carrot, chopped 2 inches
- 4 garlic cloves, bruised and left whole
- 2 fresh bay leaves
- 1 tbsp dark brown muscovado sugar
- handful fresh thyme, leaves picked
- 1 tbsp red or white wine vinegar
- 100g Comté or Emmental cheese, finely grated
- 1 tbsp wholegrain mustard
- 4 thick slices baguette, cut on the diagonal

Directions:

1. Toss the beef in the flour to coat. Heat 1 tbsp oil in a large casserole dish and add half the beef. Brown for 5 mins over a high heat, then transfer to a bowl. Splash a little of the beer into the pan and scrape up any crusty bits. Pour this over the beef. Wipe the pan clean, then repeat with the second batch of meat.

2. Then add the butter to the clean pan and cook the onions, carrot, celery and garlic for 10 mins until soft and golden. Add the bay leaves, sugar and half the thyme, cook for another minute, and finally add the vinegar.

3. Preheat the oven to gas 3, 170°C, fan 150°C. Return the beef and its juices to the pan, and pour the remaining beer over it. Cover the pan, leaving a small gap for steam to escape, and cook in the oven for 1 hr 45 mins.

4. For the croutons, mix the cheese with the mustard and remaining thyme leaves. Sprinkle a generous layer of cheese over each bread slice. Once the stew is cooked, season, stir, then top with the croutons. Cook for a further 30 mins, uncovered, until the meat is tender and the croutons are golden and bubbling.

5. Make it in a slow cooker

6. Brown the beef and veg as before, then tip into a slow cooker. Add the remaining ingredients, except those for the croutons, and use only 200ml beer. Cover and cook on a Low to Medium setting for 7 hrs. Grill the croutons on a baking sheet, and add on top of the stew to serve.

7. Freezing

8. In order to enjoy optimum flavour and quality, frozen items are best used within 3 months of their freezing date.

Slow-cooker Black-bean Soup With Turkey

👥 Servings: 6 　　🕐 Cooking Time: 6 Hours

Ingredients:

- 2 red onions, halved
- 2 tablespoons extra-virgin olive oil
- 3 medium carrots, cut into large chunks
- 4 cloves garlic, smashed
- 1 tablespoon all-purpose flour
- 1 pound dried black turtle beans, picked over, rinsed and drained
- 1 smoked turkey drumstick (1 3/4 to 2 pounds)
- 2 tablespoons pickling spice, tied in cheesecloth
- 3/4 teaspoon red pepper flakes
- Kosher salt and freshly ground pepper
- 1/2 cup chopped fresh cilantro
- Sour cream and/or lime wedges, for garnish (optional)

Directions:

1. Set aside half an onion and chop the rest. Heat the olive oil in a large skillet over medium-high heat. Add the chopped onions, carrots and garlic; sprinkle with the flour and cook, stirring, until slightly browned, 5 minutes. Add 2 tablespoons water and scrape up any browned bits from the pan. Transfer the vegetables and cooking liquid to a slow cooker. Add the beans, turkey drumstick, pickling-spice packet, red pepper flakes and 8 cups water. Cover and cook on low 6 hours.

2. Remove the drumstick and shred the meat; keep warm. Remove about 2 cups beans from the cooker and blend until smooth (or partially blend with an immersion blender). Return the beans and turkey meat to the soup. Season with salt and pepper.

3. Mince the reserved 1/2 onion. Ladle the soup into bowls and top with the cilantro and minced onion. Garnish with sour cream and lime, if desired.

Mango & Coconut Chicken Soup

👥 Servings: 6 　　🕐 Cooking Time: 6 Hours

Ingredients:

- 1 broiler/fryer chicken (3 to 4 pounds), skin removed and cut up
- 2 tablespoons canola oil
- 1 can (15 ounces) whole baby corn, drained
- 1 package (10 ounces) frozen chopped spinach, thawed
- 1 cup frozen shelled edamame, thawed
- 1 small sweet red pepper, chopped
- 1 can (13.66 ounces) light coconut milk
- 1/2 cup mango salsa
- 1 teaspoon minced fresh gingerroot
- 1 medium mango, peeled and chopped
- 2 tablespoons lime juice
- 2 green onions, chopped

Directions:

1. In a large skillet, brown chicken in oil in batches. Transfer chicken and drippings to a 5-qt. slow cooker. Add the corn, spinach, edamame and pepper. In a small bowl, combine the coconut milk, salsa and ginger; pour over vegetables.

2. Cover and cook on low for 6-8 hours or until chicken is tender. Remove chicken; cool slightly. When cool enough to handle, remove meat from bones; cut or shred meat into bite-sized pieces. Return meat to slow cooker.

3. Just before serving, stir in mango and lime juice. Sprinkle servings with green onions.

Slow Cooker Broccoli Cheese Soup

👪 Servings: 12   🕐 Cooking Time: 4 Hours

Ingredients:

- 1 lb. frozen broccoli florets
- 1 whole medium onion, diced
- 2 whole carrots, finely diced
- 5 c. low sodium chicken broth
- 2 cans cream of celery soup
- 1/4 tsp. seasoned salt
- 1/4 tsp. salt, more to taste
- 1/2 tsp. black pepper
- 1/8 tsp. cayenne pepper
- 1 1/2 lb. velveeta
- 2 c. grated sharp cheddar cheese

Directions:

1. Add the broccoli, onion, carrots, chicken broth, cream of celery soup, seasoned salt, salt, black pepper, and cayenne pepper to the slow cooker. Stir, place on the lids, and set the slow cooker on high for 4 hours.

2. After 4 hours use an immersion blender or masher to puree 3/4 of the soup. (If you use a regular blender, blend only 1 cup at a time and use extreme caution.) Add the cheese, turn the slow cooker to low, and place on the lid for 15 minutes.

3. Stir to melt the cheese and mix it in. Taste the soup and add more salt and pepper as needed.

4. Serve warm! Soup keeps great in the fridge for a couple of days.

Red Lentil, Chickpea & Chilli Soup

👪 Servings: 4   🕐 Cooking Time: 25 Mins.

Ingredients:

- 2 tsp cumin seeds
- large pinch chilli flakes
- 1 tbsp olive oil
- 1 red onion, chopped
- 140g red split lentils
- 850ml vegetable stock or water
- 400g can tomatoes, whole or chopped
- 200g can chickpeas or ½ a can, drained and rinsed (freeze leftovers)
- small bunch coriander, roughly chopped (save a few leaves, to serve)
- 4 tbsp 0% Greek yogurt, to serve

Directions:

1. Heat a large saucepan and dry-fry 2 tsp cumin seeds and a large pinch of chilli flakes for 1 min, or until they start to jump around the pan and release their aromas.

2. Add 1 tbsp olive oil and 1 chopped red onion, and cook for 5 mins.

3. Stir in 140g red split lentils, 850ml vegetable stock or water and a 400g can tomatoes, then bring to the boil. Simmer for 15 mins until the lentils have softened.

4. Whizz the soup with a stick blender or in a food processor until it is a rough purée, pour back into the pan and add a 200g can drained and rinsed chickpeas.

5. Heat gently, season well and stir in a small bunch of chopped coriander, reserving a few leaves to serve. Finish with 4 tbsp 0% Greek yogurt and extra coriander leaves.

Black Bean & Meat Stew - Feijoada

Servings: 4   **Cooking Time:** 2 Hours 20 Mins.

Ingredients:

- 250g dried black bean, soaked overnight, then drained
- 100g streaky smoked bacon, cut into slices
- 500g pork rib
- 3 chorizo cooking sausages
- 500g pork shoulder, cut into 5cm cubes
- 3 onions, chopped
- 4 garlic cloves, finely chopped
- pinch of chilli flakes
- olive oil, for cooking
- 2 bay leaves
- 2 tbsp white wine vinegar
- To serve
- steamed rice, chopped parsley or coriander, hot pepper sauce and wedges of oranges

Directions:

1. Heat a large heavy-based saucepan with a fitted lid, add the bacon and fry until crisp. Remove and keep the oil in the pan. In batches sear the ribs, sausages and pork shoulder. Season each batch with salt and pepper.
2. Remove the meat and set aside. Add the onion, garlic and chilli to the pan. Pour in a little olive oil if it needs more. Season with salt and pepper and fry for 8 mins or until soft.
3. Add the meat, bay leaves, white wine vinegar and drained beans. Cover with just enough water to cover, about 650ml. Bring to a boil and reduce the heat to a low simmer. Cover and cook for 2 hrs, or until the beans are soft and the meat is tender. If there is too much liquid in the pot take the lid off in the last hr. You can also use a slow cooker on the short method (4 hr) or make a quick version using a pressure cooker in batches for 30 mins each. Another method is to cook it in the oven for 3-4 hrs at 160C/140C fan/gas
4. Serve with rice, a sprinkle of parsley or coriander, hot pepper sauce and orange slices.

Slow Cooker Ham And Red Lentil Stew

Servings: 4   **Cooking Time:** 5 Hours

Ingredients:

- 2 tsp. olive oil
- 2 red onions, finely sliced
- 3 rosemary sprigs
- 2 x 400g tins chopped tomatoes
- 150 g red lentils, washed in cold water
- 200 g cooked ham, in a chunk if possible
- 300 g mixed roasted vegetables, in large pieces
- 700 ml hot vegetable stock
- 300 g savoy cabbage, spring greens or kale, shredded

Directions:

1. Heat oil in a large frying pan over medium heat, add onions and fry for 10min, stirring occasionally, until softened. Add rosemary and cook for a further 2min. Scrape into a slow cooker.
2. Stir in tomatoes, lentils, ham, vegetables and stock. Cover with the lid and cook on high for 4hr, or until the lentils are very tender.
3. Remove ham from the stew and shred with two forks. Return to the slow cooker along with the cabbage, greens or kale. Re-cover and cook for a further 45min, until cabbage is cooked. Remove rosemary sprigs and season generously with freshly ground black pepper and salt, if needed. Serve with crusty bread, if you like.

Slow-cooker Red Wine Beef Stew

 Servings: 8

Ingredients:

- 3 lb. beef chuck, cut into 2" pieces
- Kosher salt
- Freshly ground black pepper
- 2 tbsp. extra-virgin olive oil
- 2 tbsp. butter
- 1 2/3 c. dry red wine
- 1 tbsp. tomato paste
- 2 Yukon Gold potatoes, cut into 1" cubes
- 3 carrots, chopped into 1" pieces
- 3 celery stalks, chopped into 1" pieces
- 2 onions, chopped into quarters
- 1 c. chopped sun-dried tomatoes
- 4 cloves garlic, minced
- 1 large rosemary sprig
- 2 c. low-sodium beef broth
- 1 (28-oz.) can crushed tomatoes
- Freshly chopped parsley, for garnish

Directions:

1. In a large mixing bowl, pat beef dry with a paper towel. Season generously with salt and pepper.

2. In a large skillet over medium-high heat, heat oil. Sear meat on all sides until golden brown with a crust, working in batches if necessary, about 10 minutes. Transfer meat to slow cooker.

3. Add butter and scrape pan with a wooden spoon to loosen all browned meat bits. Stir in red wine and tomato paste; simmer for 1 minute, then transfer to slow cooker.

4. Add potatoes, carrots, celery, onions, sun-dried tomatoes, garlic, rosemary, beef broth, and crushed tomatoes to slow cooker. Season with salt and cook on high until meat is tender, 4 to 5 hours.

5. Remove stalk of rosemary. Garnish with parsley before serving.

Ginger Chicken And Quinoa Stew

Cooking Time: 3 Hours 30 Mins.

Ingredients:

- 1 cup quinoa, rinsed
- 1 medium onion, cut into 1-inch pieces
- 1 medium sweet yellow pepper, cut into 1-inch pieces
- 1 medium sweet red pepper, cut into 1-inch pieces
- 2 cups chicken broth
- 1/2 cup honey
- 1/3 cup reduced-sodium soy sauce
- 1/4 cup mirin (sweet rice wine) or sherry
- 1 tablespoon minced fresh gingerroot
- 2 garlic cloves, minced
- 1/4 to 1 teaspoon crushed red pepper flakes
- 1 can (8 ounces) unsweetened pineapple chunks, drained
- 3 green onions, thinly sliced
- 2 teaspoons sesame seeds

Directions:

1. Place the chicken in a 4- or 5-qt. slow cooker. Top with quinoa, onion and peppers. In a medium bowl, whisk the broth, honey, soy sauce, mirin, ginger, garlic and red pepper flakes; pour into slow cooker.

2. Cook, covered, on low 3-1/2 to 4 hours or until chicken is tender. Serve with pineapple, green onions and sesame seeds.

Easy Overnight Maple Bacon Pumpkin Soup

Servings: 6   **Cooking Time: 6 Hours**

Ingredients:

- 2 1/2 tbsp olive oil
- 6 middle bacon rashers, trimmed
- 1.6kg butternut pumpkin, peeled, cut into large chunks
- 2 brushed potatoes, peeled
- 1 large brown onion, chopped
- 2 tsp ground ginger

- 1 tsp mixed spice
- 3 cups salt-reduced chicken stock
- 1/2 cup thickened cream, plus extra to serve
- 2 tbsp maple syrup
- 1/4 cup chopped hazelnuts
- 2 tbsp fresh sage leaves
- Coles Bakery pane di casa bread, sliced, to serve

Directions:

1. Cut the bacon in half crossways. Cover and refrigerate streaky section of bacon until required. Heat 2 teaspoons oil in a large frying pan over medium-high heat. Cook remaining bacon for 3 minutes each side or until golden. Place bacon in a slow cooker with pumpkin, potato, onion, ginger, mixed spice and stock. Season. Cover with lid. Cook on LOW for 6 hours (or HIGH for 3 hours) or until vegetables are tender. Discard bacon.

2. Using a stick blender, blend soup until smooth. Stir in cream. Season with salt and pepper.

3. Meanwhile, preheat oven to 200C. Place a rack over a baking paper-lined baking tray. Place reserved streaky bacon on tray. Brush generously with maple syrup. Bake for 15 minutes. Turn. Cook for a further 5 minutes or until crisp. Cool 10 minutes. Break into large pieces.

4. Heat 1 tablespoon of remaining oil in a small frying pan over medium-high heat. Add hazelnuts. Cook, stirring, for 2 minutes or until lightly browned. Add sage leaves. Cook for 20 seconds or until crisp. Drain on paper towel.

5. Ladle soup among serving bowls. Drizzle with extra cream and remaining oil. Top with maple bacon, hazelnuts and sage. Serve with bread.

Slow-cooker Split Pea Soup

 Servings: 6   Cooking Time: 6 Hours

Ingredients:

- 1/2 cup chopped fresh parsley, plus 8 to 10 parsley stems
- 4 sprigs thyme
- 1 pound green split peas, picked over and rinsed
- 1 large leek, white and light green part only, halved lengthwise and thinly sliced crosswise
- 2 stalks celery, chopped
- 2 carrots, chopped
- Kosher salt and freshly ground pepper
- 1 smoked turkey leg (1 to 1 1/2 pounds)
- 1/4 cup nonfat plain yogurt
- 1/2 cup frozen peas, thawed
- Crusty multigrain bread, for serving (optional)

Directions:

1. Tie the parsley stems and thyme together with kitchen string and place in a 6-quart slow cooker. Add the split peas, leek, celery, carrots, 1 teaspoon salt and 1/2 teaspoon pepper; stir to combine. Add the turkey leg and 7 cups water. Cover and cook on low until the split peas and meat are tender, 6 to 8 hours.

2. Discard the herb bundle. Discard the skin and bones from the turkey leg and shred the meat. Vigorously stir the soup to break up the peas and make the soup smoother. Thin with water, if desired. Stir in the chopped parsley and about three-quarters of the turkey meat; season with salt and pepper.

3. Ladle the soup into bowls. Thin the yogurt with a little water, then spoon onto the soup. Top with the thawed peas and the remaining turkey. Serve with bread, if desired.

Grandma B's Bean Soup

Servings: 8   Cooking Time: 10 Hours

Ingredients:

- 1 pound dry navy beans
- 3 carrots, peeled and shredded
- 2 medium potatoes, peeled and diced
- 3 stalks celery, sliced
- 1 medium onion, diced
- 2 cups cubed cooked ham

Directions:

1. Place the beans in a slow cooker with enough water to cover, and soak 6 to 8 hours, or overnight.

2. Drain the beans, and return to the slow cooker. Cover with water, and mix in the carrots, potatoes, celery, onion, and ham.

3. Cover slow cooker, and cook soup on High for 3 1/2 hours. Switch to Low, and continue cooking at least 6 1/2 hours. The longer it cooks the more flavorful it becomes.

Slow Cooker Thai Chicken Stew Recipe

👥 Servings: 4-6   🕐 Cooking Time: 4 Hours-8 Hours

Ingredients:

- 5 chicken drumsticks
- 5 chicken thighs
- 1tbsp vegetable oil
- 4tbsp red curry paste
- 2tbsp soft brown sugar
- juice of half a lemon
- 1 tbsp Worcestershire sauce

- 2tbsp fish sauce
- 2 limes zested and juiced
- 1 x 400g tins coconut milk
- 125ml vegetable or chicken stock
- To serve
- handful chopped fresh coriander

Directions:

1. Turn on the slow cooker. Heat a large frying pan with the vegetable oil. Season the chicken pieces and brown on all sides. Remove and place in the slow cooker.

2. Sauté the curry paste for 2 minutes in the frying pan. Add the brown sugar, lemon juice and Worcestershire sauce and let the sugar melt. Pour in the coconut milk, stock, lime zest and juice and the fish sauce. Mix together and pour over the chicken in the slow cooker. Cook for 4 hours (high) or 8 hours (slow) until the chicken is cooked through with no pink showing.

3. Serve the chicken stew over warm basmati rice with chopped fresh coriander and sliced red chillies.

Huevos Rancheros Slow Cooker Stew

👥 Servings: 4   🕐 Cooking Time: 6 Hours 30 Mins.

Ingredients:

- FOR THE STEW
- 1 onion, finely chopped
- 2 mixed coloured peppers, deseeded and finely sliced
- 1 tbsp. chipotle paste, we used Sainsbury's own
- 2 tsp. garlic granules
- 1 tsp. ground cumin
- 2 tsp. ground coriander
- 2 tsp. dried oregano

- 1 vegetable stock cube, crumbled
- 2 x 400g tins black beans, drained and rinsed
- 200 g cherry tomatoes, halved
- 1 tsp. cornflour
- TO GARNISH AND SERVE, OPTIONAL
- Small handful coriander, roughly chopped
- 1 small avocado, sliced
- Corn tortillas taco wraps

Directions:

1. Mix all of the stew ingredients, reserving some of the cherry tomatoes for garnish, into the bowl of the slow cooker. Add a generous amount of seasoning and mix well. Cook on low for 6hr.

2. After 6hr, crack eggs into the top of the stew, spacing apart. Recover and cook on low for 25min, until the whites of the eggs and set and yolks are still runny.

3. Divide between 4 bowls, squeeze over the lime, top with feta and reserved cherry tomatoes. Garnish with coriander and avocado, if using. Serve with corn tortillas wraps, if you like.

SNACKS AND APPETIZERS RECIPES

Rotel Dip

👪 Servings: 12   🕐 Cooking Time: 2 Hours

Ingredients:

- 1 lb. ground beef
- 16 oz. Velveeta cheese this is the smaller box
- 20 oz. Rotel® diced Tomatoes with & Green Chiles (TWO 10-oz. cans) DO NOT DRAIN
- 2 tsp. chili powder
- 1/4 tsp. garlic powder
- For serving
- corn chips
- chopped cilantro optional

Directions:

1. Set a large skillet over medium high heat on the stove top. Brown and crumble the ground beef, drain the fat.
2. Add the cooked ground beef to the slow cooker, cube the velveeta and add on top of the beef.
3. Pour over the can of rotel and sprinkle over the chili and garlic powder. Stir.
4. Place the lid on the slow cooker. Cook on HIGH for 2 hours or until cheese is melted and the dip is hot.
5. Keep on warm while serving.

Notes:

1. How can I make this less spicy?
2. Rotel tends to be spicy (even the original style), be sure to use "Mild" if you have any aversion to spicy food.
3. Alternatively, you can use mild salsa instead of Rotel.
4. Can I use sausage instead of ground beef?
5. Ground sausage is great in this recipe!
6. I like to use 1 pound of Jimmy Dean Breakfast sausage.
7. How can I thin the dip after it's been on the warm setting for too long?
8. The dip will thicken with time if left on the warm setting for a length of time while serving.
9. Add a splash of milk to thin the dip.

Slow Cooker Candied Kielbasa

👪 Servings: 12   🕐 Cooking Time: 5 Hours

Ingredients:

- 28 oz. kielbasa (two 14-oz. pkgs)
- ¾ cup ketchup
- ¼ cup horseradish creamed or prepared
- horseradish (I use Beaver Hot Cream Horseradish)
- 1 cup brown sugar

Directions:

1. Cut the kielbasa into 1 inch slices. (not at an angle, straight down cuts).
2. Add to the slow cooker.
3. Add the ketchup, horseradish and brown sugar.
4. Stir.
5. Cook on HIGH for 3 hours, or LOW for 5 hours stirring occasionally. You want to cook these longer than just heating for kielbasa will start soaking the sauce up the longer it cooks.

Notes:

1. Add any leftover sausage to an airtight container and keep it in the fridge for up to 5 days. You can reheat them in a pan on the stovetop over medium-low heat.
2. To keep warm at a party, use the "Keep Warm" setting, so the sausage and sauce don't continue cooking. These will stay good for about 2-3 hours if you stir occasionally.

Slow Cooker Beef And Rice Enchilada Dip

👪 Servings: 8   🕐 Cooking Time: 2 Hours

Ingredients:

- 1 lb. ground beef
- 1 cup diced white onion
- 1/4 tsp. salt
- 1/4 tsp. pepper
- 3 cups shredded cheddar cheese divided
- 1 cup sour cream
- 10 oz. can red enchilada sauce
- 15 oz. can pinto beans drained
- 2 1/2 cups cooked white rice
- 8 oz. can sliced black olives drained
- 2 Roma tomatoes diced
- Tortilla Chips for serving

Directions:

1. Brown the ground beef and onion together, do this directly in the slow cooker if you have a Multi-Cooker, or brown the meat in a skillet on the stove. Drain the fat from the meat, add the meat to the slow cooker (if you browned it on the stove).
2. Sprinkle the meat with the salt and pepper.
3. Add half of the cheese, sour cream, pinto beans, and rice to the meat. Stir, then flatten out. Sprinkle with remaining cheese.
4. Cover and cook on HIGH for 2 hours, without opening the lid during the cooking time.
5. When the cooking time is through, sprinkle on the olives and tomatoes. Serve with tortilla chips and enjoy!

Sweet Baby Ray's Pulled Pork Chow Down

 Servings: 8   Cooking Time: 8 Hours

Ingredients:

- 5 pounds pork shoulder
- 1/2 tsp. pepper
- 1/2 tsp. salt
- 1/2 tsp. onion powder
- 1/4 tsp. garlic powder
- 1 tsp. paprika
- 2 Tbsp. cooking oil vegetable or canola
- 1/2 cup diced sweet onion
- 1/4 cup chopped cilantro
- 2 tsp. diced jalapeno leave out if you don't like spicy
- 1 cup Sweet Baby Ray's Original Barbecue Sauce
- 1 cup Apple Cider
- For Serving the Chow Downs:
- Prepared Cornbread I made a double batch of store bought cornbread mix in a 9x13 pan
- Sweet Baby Ray's Barbecue Sauce
- Sour cream
- Shredded sharp cheddar cheese
- Diced sweet onion

Directions:

1. In a small bowl combine the pepper, salt, onion powder, garlic powder and paprika. Remove the pork from its packaging and pat dry with a paper towel.
2. Sprinkle the seasoning mix you just made onto the pork roast.
3. Set a large skillet to medium-high heat.
4. Add enough oil to coat the bottom of the pan. Sear the roast on all sides.
5. Place the seasoned pork roast into a 6-quart slow cooker.
6. Add the onion, cilantro, jalapeno Sweet Baby Ray's Barbecue Sauce to the top of the roast. Add the apple cider around the roast.
7. Cover, and cook on LOW for 8 hours.
8. Shred the meat with 2 fork right in the slow cooker, discarding any fat.
9. Serve the shredded pork over cornbread topped with Sweet Baby Ray's Barbecue Sauce, sour cream, cheese, sweet onion, cilantro and jalapenos.

Pesto Mashed Potatoes

Servings: 12

Ingredients:

- 4-1/2 pounds red potatoes, cut into 1-inch pieces
- 6 tablespoons butter, cubed
- 1-1/2 teaspoons salt
- 3/4 teaspoon pepper
- 1 to 1-1/3 cups heavy whipping cream, warmed
- 1/3 cup prepared pesto
- 1/4 cup extra virgin olive oil

Directions:

1. Place potatoes in a large saucepan or Dutch oven and cover with water. Bring to a boil. Reduce heat; cover and cook for 10-15 minutes or until tender. Drain. Mash potatoes with butter, salt, pepper and enough cream to achieve desired consistency. Transfer potatoes to a serving dish; swirl pesto into potatoes. Drizzle with olive oil; serve immediately.

Slow Cooker Turmeric And Coconut Dhal

Servings: 4　　　**Cooking Time: 6 Hours 5 Mins.**

Ingredients:

- 400ml coconut milk
- 3/4 cup (150g) yellow split peas
- 3/4 cup (150g) French-style lentils
- 1/4 cup (50g) quinoa, rinsed, drained
- 4 cups (1L) salt-reduced vegetable stock
- 2 brown onions, chopped
- 4 garlic cloves, bruised
- 2cm-piece ginger, peeled, thinly sliced
- 4 stems curry leaves
- 1 large sweet potato, chopped
- 1 tbsp garam masala
- 1/4 tsp ground cloves
- 1/4 tsp ground cinnamon
- 2 tsp ground turmeric
- 300g green beans, halved lengthways
- 1/3 cup (15g) coconut flakes, toasted

Directions:

1. Reserve ¼ cup (60ml) coconut milk. Place remaining coconut milk in a slow cooker with split peas, lentils, quinoa, stock, onion, garlic, ginger, curry leaf stems, sweet potato, garam masala, cloves, cinnamon and turmeric. Cover. Cook for 6 hours on high (or 8 hours on low) or until peas are tender and mixture thickens. Discard curry leaf stems.
2. Cook the beans in a large saucepan of boiling water for 2-3 mins or until bright green and tender. Drain. Season.
3. Divide the lentil mixture evenly among serving bowls. Top with the beans and sprinkle with the coconut flakes. Drizzle with the reserved coconut milk.

Notes:

1. SERVE WITH fried curry leaf stems, coriander sprigs, lime wedges and mini pappadums.

Slow Cooker Shredded Beef Sheet Tray Nachos

Servings: 8   **Cooking Time: 6 Hours**

Ingredients:

- 3 lbs. beef chuck roast
- 1/2 tsp. salt
- 1/4 tsp. pepper
- 1/4 tsp. onion powder
- 2 Tbsp. vegetable oil
- 20 oz. Rotel diced tomatoes with green peppers (two-10 oz. cans) Use original, mild or hot
- 1 sweet yellow onion diced
- 1 1/4 oz. taco seasoning packet (I like mild McCormick for this recipe)
- To assemble nachos:
- 11 oz. bag tortilla chips

- 1 lb. Monterey Jack cheese shredded
- Additional topping ideas:
- sour cream
- salsa
- sliced avocado or guacamole
- minced green or sweet onion
- diced Roma tomato
- hot sauce
- salsa
- sliced black olives
- chopped cilantro

Directions:

1. For the meat:
2. Sprinkle the roast with the salt, pepper and onion powder.
3. Heat a large skillet on the stove-top to medium-high heat, once hot, add the oil.
4. Brown the roast on all sides and transfer to the slow cooker.
5. Add the Rotel, onions, and taco seasoning on top of the roast.
6. Cover and cook on HIGH for 6 hours, or LOW for 8-10 hours, without opening the lid during the cooking time. Opening the lid during the cooking time lets heat escape and can cause the meat not to tenderize.
7. After the meat is done cooking, pre-heat the oven to BROIL.
8. Shred the meat with 2 forks, discard any fatty pieces. (I shred the meat right in the slow cooker to save on dirtying an extra plate).
9. Assembling the Nachos:
10. Add the entire bag of chips to a sheet pan.
11. Add the shredded beef to the chips in an even layer, then the cheese.
12. Put the nachos in the oven, it will take about 5 minutes for the cheese to melt.
13. Add desired toppings or serve them on the side and let guests choose what they want.

Notes:

1. How can I make this less spicy?
2. Use a can of diced tomatoes or mild salsa instead of Rotel. Rotel tends to be on the spicy side.
3. What is the best cheese for nachos?
4. We love Monterey Jack cheese for nachos. Monterey Jack cheese melts very well and is very mild in flavor.

Super Bowl Nacho Bar

Servings: 12   **Cooking Time:** 2 Hours

Ingredients:

- Nacho Cheese Ingredients:
- 2 lb. box original Velveeta cheese (or buy a large can of nacho cheese)
- 1 cup mild La Victoria taco sauce
- 1 cup sour cream
- milk for thinning
- Other Ingredients:
- 2 lbs. ground beef cooked and seasoned
- 16 oz. jar salsa
- 4 tomatoes chopped
- 16 oz. jar jalapeno slices
- 2 bunches of green onions sliced
- 16 oz. sour cream
- 3 small cans of sliced black olives
- 30 oz. black beans drained (two 15-oz. cans)
- 2 large bags of tortilla chips
- Guacamole Ingredients:
- 5 avocados 1
- 1/4 cup sour cream
- 1 lime
- salt to tase

Directions:

1. Cube the velveeta, put in slow cooker with 1 cup of sour cream, and 1 cup of taco sauce. Cook on high for 1 1/2 to 2 hours, stir often. Add milk to thin. You don't want the cheese to be gloppy. I kept the cheese on high during the party, so the cheese would stay thinned out, stir often, and keep adding milk if the cheese thickens.

2. Guacamole directions:

3. Take 4 to 5 avocados, and mash with a fork and add 1/4 cup sour cream, 2 tablespoons lime juice, and a dash of salt, mix lightly.

4. Assemble Nacho Bar:

5. Put the cooked and seasoned ground beef in a small slow cooker on low, or a pan with a lid works fine. Put all your toppings in little dishes (I got mine at the dollar store, they came with lids). Put the chips in a big bowl. I got the white paper nacho trays from a restaurant supply store (Cash and Carry), but you can get them at Costco too. Invite all your friends over for the big game, I think they will be impressed!

6. this can be doubled if you're expecting more people

Slow Cooker Artichoke Dip

👥 Servings: 10   🕐 Cooking Time: 1 Hours 30 Mins.

Ingredients:

- 8 oz. pkg. cream cheese room temperature
- 1 cup sour cream
- ½ cup mayo
- 1.8 oz. pkg. leek soup mix (Knorr brand) Knorr vegetable soup mix works great too!
- 2 garlic cloves minced
- 1 Tbsp. lemon juice
- ¼ tsp. pepper
- 28 oz. canned artichokes drained and chopped (two 14-oz. cans)
- 1 ½ cup shredded parmesan cheese divided
- French bread for serving

Directions:

1. In a large bowl, stir together the cream cheese, sour cream, and mayo.
2. Fold in soup mix, garlic, lemon juice, pepper, artichokes, and one cup of the cheese.
3. Spray a 4-quart or larger slow cooker with non-stick spray, and spread the dip down in an even layer, top with remaining cheese.
4. Cover, and cook on HIGH for 1.5 - 2 hours.
5. Serve with soft french bread. Enjoy!

Notes:

1. Store any remaining dip in an airtight container and keep it in the fridge for up to 3 days. You can reheat it on the stovetop over medium-low heat until warmed throughout.
2. Want to add spinach? Go ahead! Add one small box of thawed frozen spinach (drained VERY well).

Slow Cooker Spinach Artichoke Dip Recipe

Servings: 10   **Cooking Time: 3 Hours**

Ingredients:

- 12 oz. bag frozen chopped spinach (or a 10 oz. box) THAWED and drained VERY well, see Directions below
- 1 bunch green onions sliced
- 16 oz. cream cheese (two 8-oz. boxes)
- 16 oz. sour cream
- 8 oz. pkg. shredded mozzarella cheese (2 cups)

- 1 cup shredded Parmesan cheese
- 1 tsp. salt
- 1/2 tsp. onion powder
- 1/4 tsp. pepper
- 5 garlic cloves finely minced
- 28 oz. canned quartered artichokes (optional) chopped roughly and drained well

Directions:

1. The water from the spinach needs to be removed. Do this by adding the thawed spinach to a clean tea towel or dish towel. Gather the towel around the spinach and wring out the liquid into the sink or a bowl.

2. Add the strained spinach to the slow cooker. Add the remaining ingredients. Stir. You won't be able to mix this all the way, that's ok. Just a rough stir is fine.

3. Place the lid on the slow cooker. Cook on HIGH for 2.5-3 hours or LOW for 4 hours. Stirring occasionally. The dip is done when it is piping hot.

Notes:

1. What do I serve this with?
2. Homemade tortilla Chips or Tostito scoops
3. French bread slices
4. Pita Chips
5. Veggies such as carrots or celery
6. Can I use fresh spinach?
7. Yes! Use 4 cups of fresh baby spinach in this . Add at the beginning of the cooking time.
8. Can I make this ahead of time?
9. Yes, you can prepare this the day ahead of time then cook in the slow cooker when you are ready.
10. Variations
11. Sun-dried tomato - Add a 1/4 cup of chopped sundried tomatoes for a tangy twist in this .
12. Lemony - Add the juice of 1/2 of a lemon to this dish to add depth of flavor.
13. Spicy - Add two small cans of fire-roasted peppers or one chopped jalapeno with its seeds.

VEGETABLES & VEGETARIAN RECIPES

Vegetarian Chili With Grains And Beans

Servings: 8

Ingredients:

- 1 (28-ounce) can fire-roasted crushed tomatoes
- 1 (14.5-ounce) can petite-diced tomatoes
- 1 tbsp. chili powder
- 2 tsp. ground cumin
- 1 tsp. ground coriander
- 3 cloves garlic, pressed
- 1 onion, chopped
- 1 large carrot, chopped
- 1 large poblano pepper, chopped
- 3/4 c. wheat berries
- Kosher salt and freshly ground black pepper
- 1 (15.5-ounce) can black beans, rinsed
- 1 (15.5-ounce) can kidney beans, rinsed
- Sour cream, grated Cheddar cheese, sliced scallions, fresh cilantro, and lime wedges, for serving

Directions:

1. Combine crushed tomatoes, diced tomatoes, chili powder, cumin, coriander, garlic, onion, carrot, poblano, wheat berries, and 3/4 cup water in a 5- to 6-quart slow cooker. Season with salt and pepper. Cook, covered, until wheat berries are cooked but still chewy, 7 to 8 hours on low or 5 to 6 hours on high.
2. Stir in both beans and cook until warmed through, 8 to 10 minutes. Serve with sour cream, Cheddar, scallions, cilantro, and lime wedges alongside.

5-a-day Tagine

Servings: 4   **Cooking Time:** 35 Mins.

Ingredients:

- 4 carrots, cut into chunks
- 4 small parsnips, or 3 large, cut into chunks
- 3 red onions, cut into wedges
- 2 red peppers, deseeded and cut into chunks
- 2 tbsp olive oil
- 1 tsp each ground cumin, paprika, cinnamon and mild chilli powder
- 400g can chopped tomato
- 2 small handfuls soft dried apricots
- 2 tsp honey

Directions:

1. rections:
2. Heat oven to 200C/fan 180C/gas 6. Scatter the veg over a couple of baking trays, drizzle with half the oil, season, then rub the oil over the veg with your hands to coat. Roast for 30 mins until tender and beginning to brown.
3. Meanwhile, fry the spices in the remaining oil for 1 min – they should sizzle and start to smell aromatic. Tip in the tomatoes, apricots, honey and a can of water. Simmer for 5 mins until the sauce is slightly reduced and the apricots plump, then stir in the veg and some seasoning. Serve with couscous or jacket potatoes.

Notes:

1. IF YOU WANT TO USE A SLOW COOKER...
2. Give this Moroccan one pot some extra time. Mix the vegetables, oil, spices, tomatoes, can of water, apricots and honey in your slow cooker, cover and cook on Low for 6-8 hours until the veg is tender.

Slow Cooker Vegetable Lasagne

 Servings: 6   Cooking Time: 2 Hours 30 Mins-3 Hours.

Ingredients:

- 1 tbsp rapeseed oil
- 2 onions, sliced
- 2 large garlic cloves, chopped
- 2 large courgettes, diced (400g)
- 1 red and 1 yellow pepper, deseeded and roughly sliced
- 400g can chopped tomatoes
- 2 tbsp tomato purée
- 2 tsp vegetable bouillon
- 15g fresh basil, chopped plus a few leaves
- 1 large aubergine, sliced across length or width for maximum surface area
- 6 wholewheat lasagne sheets (105g)
- 125g vegetarian buffalo mozzarella, chopped

Directions:

1. Heat 1 tbsp rapeseed oil in a large non-stick pan and fry 2 sliced onions and 2 chopped large garlic cloves for 5 mins, stirring frequently until softened.

2. Tip in 2 diced large courgettes, 1 red and 1 yellow pepper, both roughly sliced, and 400g chopped tomatoes with 2 tbsp tomato purée, 2 tsp vegetable bouillon and 15g chopped basil.

3. Stir well, cover and cook for 5 mins. Don't be tempted to add more liquid as plenty of moisture will come from the vegetables once they start cooking.

4. Slice 1 large aubergine. Lay half the slices of aubergine in the base of the slow cooker and top with 3 sheets of lasagne.

5. Add a third of the ratatouille mixture, then the remaining aubergine slices, 3 more lasagne sheets, then the remaining ratatouille mixture.

6. Cover and cook on High for 2½ - 3 hours until the pasta and vegetables are tender. Turn off the machine.

7. Scatter 125g vegetarian buffalo mozzarella over the vegetables then cover and leave for 10 mins to settle and melt the cheese.

8. Scatter with extra basil and serve with a handful of rocket.

Sun-dried Tomato Spinach-artichoke Dip

 Servings: 3   Cooking Time: 2 Hours

Ingredients:

- 1 package (10 ounces) frozen chopped spinach, thawed and squeezed dry
- 1 package (8 ounces) cream cheese, softened
- 1 cup shredded smoked Gouda cheese
- 1/2 cup shredded fontina cheese
- 1/2 cup chopped water-packed artichoke hearts
- 1/4 to 1/2 cup soft sun-dried tomato halves (not packed in oil), chopped
- 1/3 cup finely chopped onion
- 1 garlic clove, minced
- Assorted fresh vegetables and crackers

Directions:

1. In a 1-1/2-qt. slow cooker, mix spinach, cheeses, artichokes, sun-dried tomatoes, onion and garlic. Cook, covered, on low until cheese is melted, 2-3 hours. Stir before serving. Serve with vegetables and crackers.

Slow Cooker Garlicky Mashed Potatoes

 Servings: 8

Ingredients:

- Cooking spray
- 3 lb. baby potatoes, quartered
- 4 tbsp. butter
- 3 cloves garlic, minced
- 1/4 c. water
- Kosher salt
- Freshly ground black pepper
- 1/3 c. sour cream
- 1/4 c. milk
- 1 tsp. dried oregano
- 1/2 tsp. dried rosemary
- 1 tbsp. chives, for garnish

Directions:

1. Grease the inside of your slow cooker with cooking spray. Add potatoes, butter, garlic, and water to slow cooker. Season with salt and pepper. Stir, cover, and cook on high heat for 3 hours, or until potatoes are tender.
2. Once potatoes are tender, add sour cream, milk and spices. Mash with a potato masher and season with more salt and pepper, to taste.
3. Garnish with chives before serving.

Slow Cooker Winter Vegetables With Coconut Milk And Sambal

Servings: 6-8   Cooking Time: 4 Hours.

Ingredients:

- 1 (2 3/4 pound) butternut squash, unpeeled, quartered, and cut into 2-inch chunks
- 4 (about 2 pounds) sweet potatoes, peeled and cut into 2-inch chunks
- 10 ounces shiitake mushrooms, stemmed and halved
- 1 bunch scallions (green and white parts separated), cut into 1-inch pieces
- 2 (14-ounce) cans coconut milk
- 1 1/2 cups water
- 3 tablespoons soy sauce
- 2 teaspoons sambal oelek, or other Asian chili paste
- 1 teaspoon kosher salt
- 1 cup cilantro leaves, roughly chopped for garnish
- 1/4 cup salted peanuts, roughly chopped for garnish

Directions:

1. Toss the squash, potatoes, shiitakes, and scallions whites together in the slow cooker. Whisk the coconut milk, water, soy sauce, sambal, and salt together in a bowl; then pour over the vegetables. Cover and cook on HIGH for 4 hours, or until tender.
2. Evenly divide the vegetables and broth into warm bowls. Scatter the scallion greens, cilantro, and peanuts on top and serve.

Grandma's Slow Cooker Vegetarian Chili

 Servings: 8   🕐 Cooking Time: 2 Hours

Ingredients:

- 1 (19 ounce) can black bean soup
- 1 (15 ounce) can kidney beans, rinsed and drained
- 1 (15 ounce) can garbanzo beans, rinsed and drained
- 1 (16 ounce) can vegetarian baked beans
- 1 (14.5 ounce) can chopped tomatoes in puree
- 1 (15 ounce) can whole kernel corn, drained
- 1 onion, chopped
- 1 green bell pepper, chopped
- 2 stalks celery, chopped
- 2 cloves garlic, chopped
- 1 tablespoon chili powder, or to taste
- 1 tablespoon dried parsley
- 1 tablespoon dried oregano
- 1 tablespoon dried basil

Directions:

1. Combine black bean soup, kidney beans, garbanzo beans, baked beans, tomatoes, corn, onion, bell pepper, and celery. Season with garlic, chili powder, parsley, oregano, and basil.

2. Cook on High for at least 2 hours.

Slow Cooker Cheesy Creamed Greens

 Servings: 6-8   🕐 Cooking Time: 3 Hours 10 Mins.

Ingredients:

- 50g butter
- ½ tbsp olive oil
- 1 onion, thinly sliced
- 400g cavolo nero
- 3 leeks, sliced
- 100ml stock
- 400ml double cream
- 1 heaped tsp Dijon mustard
- generous grating of nutmeg
- 40g grated parmesan or vegetarian alternative

Directions:

1. Heat the slow cooker to low. Heat the butter and oil in a frying pan. Add the onion and fry for 5 mins over a low heat until softened and translucent. Add the cavolo nero to the pan and fry for 5 mins or until beginning to wilt. Tip into the slow cooker along with the leeks, stock and 300ml of the cream. Cook with the lid on for 3 hrs, stirring occasionally.

2. Stir through the remaining cream, the mustard, nutmeg and cheese, as well as some seasoning just before serving. Will keep, covered, in the fridge for up to three days. Reheat in the slow cooker on medium for 45 mins-1 hr.

Slow Cooker Mushroom And Bean Hotpot

 Servings: 6   Cooking Time: 3 Hours 15 Mins.

Ingredients:

- 3 tbsp. olive oil
- 700 g (1½lb) chestnut mushrooms, roughly chopped
- 1 large onion, finely chopped
- 2 tbsp. plain flour
- 2 tbsp. mild curry paste
- 150 ml (¼ pint) dry white wine
- 400 g tin chopped tomatoes
- 2 tbsp. sun-dried tomato paste
- 2 × 400 g × 400g tins mixed beans, drained and rinsed
- 3 tbsp. mango chutney
- 3 tbsp. freshly chopped coriander and mint leaves

Directions:

1. Heat the oil in a large pan over a medium heat. Add the mushrooms and onion and fry for 8-10min until the vegetables are just softened and golden. Stir in the flour and curry paste and cook for 1-2min, then add the wine, chopped tomatoes, tomato paste and beans.
2. Bring to the boil, then carefully transfer mixture to a slow cooker, cover and cook on Low for 2-3hr.
3. Stir in the mango chutney and chopped herbs and serve with rice or naan bread.

Pesto Vegetable Pizza

Servings: 6

Ingredients:

- 1 prebaked 12-inch thin pizza crust
- 2 garlic cloves, halved
- 1/2 cup pesto sauce
- 3/4 cup packed fresh spinach, chopped
- 2 large portobello mushrooms, thinly sliced
- 1 medium sweet yellow pepper, julienned
- 2 plum tomatoes, seeded and sliced
- 1/3 cup packed fresh basil, chopped
- 1 cup shredded part-skim mozzarella cheese
- 1/4 cup grated Parmesan cheese
- 1/2 teaspoon fresh or dried oregano

Directions:

1. Preheat oven to 450°. Place crust on an ungreased 12-in. pizza pan. Rub cut side of garlic cloves over crust; discard garlic. Spread pesto sauce over crust. Top with spinach, mushrooms, yellow pepper, tomatoes and basil. Sprinkle with cheeses and oregano.
2. Bake until pizza is heated through and cheese is melted, 10-15 minutes.

POULTRY RECIPES

Chicken And Bacon Casserole

Servings: 4   Cooking Time: 6 Hours

Ingredients:

- 1 kg chicken breast fillets diced
- 100 g bacon rashers roughly chopped
- 3 potatoes large thickly sliced
- 2 carrots sliced
- 50 g French onion soup mix
- 1 tbs mixed herbs dried
- 3/4 cup water
- 1/4 cup Bulla Cooking Cream

Directions:

1. Brown chicken and bacon before adding to the slow cooker if you prefer. Layer potatoes and carrots on the bottom of slow cooker.

2. Add chicken and bacon on top.

3. Mix soup and herbs together with water.

4. Add to slow cooker. Cook on high for 4 hours, or low for 6-8 hours.

5. Stir through cooking cream 10 minutes before serving.

Notes:

1. You can also use chicken thigh fillets.

2. Serve with steamed broccoli or beans.

3. May require extra water, depending on your slow cooker.

Slow Cooker Honey Garlic Chicken And Veggies

Servings: 4   **Cooking Time: 8 Hours 5 Mins.**

Ingredients:

- 8 bone-in, skin-on chicken thighs
- 16 ounces baby red potatoes, halved
- 16 ounces baby carrots
- 16 ounces green beans, trimmed
- 2 tablespoons chopped fresh parsley leaves
- FOR THE SAUCE
- 1/2 cup reduced sodium soy sauce

- 1/2 cup honey
- 1/4 cup ketchup
- 2 cloves garlic, minced
- 1 teaspoon dried basil
- 1/2 teaspoon dried oregano
- 1/4 teaspoon crushed red pepper flakes
- 1/4 teaspoon ground black pepper

Directions:

1. In a large bowl, combine soy sauce, honey, ketchup, garlic, basil, oregano, red pepper flakes and pepper.
2. Place chicken thighs, potatoes, carrots and soy sauce mixture into a 6-qt slow cooker. Cover and cook on low heat for 7-8 hours or high for 3-4 hours, basting every hour. Add green beans during the last 30 minutes of cooking time.
3. OPTIONAL: Preheat oven to broil. Place chicken thighs onto a baking sheet, skin side up, and broil until crisp, about 3-4 minutes.
4. Serve chicken immediately with potatoes, carrots and green beans, garnished with parsley, if desired.

Green Chicken & Vegetable Curry

Servings: 4   **Cooking Time: 20 Mins.**

Ingredients:

- 2 tbsp sunflower oil
- 500g boneless, skinless chicken thigh, cut into bite-size pieces
- 1-2 tbsp Thai green curry paste
- 2 small parsnips, cut into chunks
- 400g can coconut milk

- 1 tbsp fish sauce
- 2 tsp light muscovado sugar
- 100g mushrooms, sliced
- handful frozen peas
- handful basil leaves, torn

Directions:

1. Heat the oil in a large pan, add the chicken and fry until lightly coloured. Stir in the curry paste to coat the chicken. Add the parsnips, coconut milk, fish sauce and sugar, then bring to a gentle simmer, stirring every now and then.
2. Reduce the heat, cover the pan and cook for 10 mins. Add the mushrooms and peas, then cook for a further 5 mins until the chicken and vegetables are tender. Scatter with basil to serve.
3. If you want to use a slow cooker, cook the chicken in a frying pan until lightly coloured, then tip into your slow cooker and coat in the curry sauce. Add the parsnips, coconut milk, fish sauce and sugar, then cover and cook on High for 3-5 hours. Check the chicken is tender, then add the mushrooms and peas and cook for a further 30 mins.

Slow Cooker Buffalo Chicken Chili

Servings: 4-6   **Cooking Time:** 4 Hours

Ingredients:

- 1 tablespoon olive oil
- 1 sweet onion diced
- 1/2 cup diced celery
- 1 14 ounce jar roasted red peppers, drained and chopped
- 4 garlic cloves minced
- 1 tablespoon smoked paprika
- 1 tablespoon chili powder
- 2 teaspoons ground cumin
- 1/2 teaspoon salt
- 1/2 teaspoon black pepper
- 2 cups cooked and shredded chicken
- 1/2 cup beer
- 1 28 ounce can crushed tomatoes
- 1 14 ounce can fire roasted diced tomatoes
- 3/4 cup buffalo wing sauce
- 2 14 ounce cans pinto beans, drained and rinsed
- 1 14 ounce can cannellini beans, drained and rinsed
- FOR TOPPING:
- extra wing sauce
- grated sharp cheddar
- crumbled blue cheese
- sliced green onions
- freshly sliced chives
- lime wedges for spritzing
- avocado slices

Directions:

1. Note: my slow cooker has the ability to sear and sauté, so I can do everything in the cooker. If yours does not do this, sauté the veggies in another pot on the stove, or just add everything into the slow cooker together and don't worry about sauteing the veg!

2. Heat the olive oil in your slow cooker or in a saucepan over medium heat. Add the onions, celery, red peppers and garlic and stir. Stir in the paprika, chili powder, cumin, salt and pepper. Cook until the veggies soften slightly. Stir in the cooked, shredded chicken. Add in the beer and let it simmer until it reduces by about half. At this point, either transfer the mixture to your slow cooker or turn your slow cooker to the low setting. Add the crushed tomatoes, fire roasted tomatoes, wing sauce, pinto beans and cannellini beans. Cover and cook on low for however long you need – since the chicken is cooked, this chili is technically "done," but letting it cook for a few hours will deepen the flavor! I like to cook it for about 4 hours on low, but you can cook it for 2 hours or even 8 hours – whatever you have. I would just keep it on the low.

3. When it comes time to serve, serve in bowls with toppings of extra wing sauce, grated cheddar cheese, crumbled blue cheese, green onions, chives, avocado and lime wedges!

Notes:

1. Also, if you prefer the ground meat texture to chili over shredded chicken, brown 1 pound of ground chicken with the veggies and use that as your meat instead!

Brown Sugar Bbq Chicken

 Servings: 6   Cooking Time: Mins.

Ingredients:

- 2 lb. boneless skinless chicken breasts
- 1 c. barbecue sauce, plus more for serving
- 1/2 c. packed light or brown sugar
- 1/4 c. bourbon
- 1/4 c. Italian dressing
- 2 tsp. garlic powder
- 1 tsp. paprika
- Kosher salt
- Freshly ground black pepper
- 6 potato buns
- Coleslaw, for serving

Directions:

1. In a slow-cooker, combine chicken breasts, barbecue sauce, brown sugar, bourbon, Italian dressing, garlic powder and paprika. Season with salt and pepper.
2. Toss until well coated, then cover and cook on high for 4 hours or on low for 6 hours.
3. Shred chicken and serve on buns with a drizzle of barbecue sauce and a spoonful of coleslaw.

Leek And Herb Stuffed Chicken

Servings: 4   Cooking Time: 35 Mins.

Ingredients:

- 3 medium leeks (white and light green portions only), cleaned and chopped
- 1 tablespoon olive oil
- 1/2 teaspoon dried rosemary, crushed
- 1/2 teaspoon dried thyme
- 1/4 teaspoon salt
- 1/4 teaspoon pepper
- 4 boneless skinless chicken breast halves (6 ounces each)
- PECAN CRUST:
- 1/4 cup finely chopped pecans
- 1/4 cup dry bread crumbs
- 1/4 teaspoon dried rosemary, crushed
- 1/4 teaspoon dried thyme
- 1/2 teaspoon salt
- 1/4 teaspoon pepper
- 1/4 cup Dijon mustard
- 1 tablespoon olive oil

Directions:

1. In a small skillet, saute leeks in oil until almost tender. Add the rosemary, thyme, salt and pepper; saute 1 minute longer. Remove from the heat; cool.
2. Flatten each chicken breast half to 1/4-in. thickness; top with leek mixture. Roll up and secure with toothpicks.
3. In a small shallow bowl, combine the pecans, bread crumbs, rosemary, thyme, salt and pepper. Brush mustard over chicken, then coat with pecan mixture. Place seam side down in a greased 11x7-in. baking dish. Drizzle with oil.
4. Bake, uncovered, at 375° for 35-40 minutes or until the chicken is no longer pink. Discard toothpicks.

Creamy Slow Cooker Goulash Chicken

👥 Servings: 4   🕐 Cooking Time: 10 Mins.

Ingredients:

- 500g baby red potatoes, halved
- 400g can cherry tomatoes
- 300ml thickened cream
- 3 tsp smoked paprika
- 1 batch Freeze and save one-pot big-batch chicken
- Crème fraiche, to serve (optional)
- Chopped continental parsley, to serve (optional)
- Steamed broccoli, to serve (see below)

Directions:

1. Cook the potatoes in a large saucepan of boiling water for 10 minutes or until just tender. Drain and run under cold running water. Drain. Combine the potatoes, tomatoes, cream and paprika in an airtight container. Place in the freezer.

2. Defrost the potato mixture (see tips). Place in a large saucepan with a batch of the defrosted chicken. Cook on medium-high heat, stirring occasionally for 5 minutes to gently reheat.

3. Either stir the broccoli through the goulash mixture and cook, uncovered, for a further 3 minutes or until warmed through or place the broccoli in a microwave-safe container and microwave until defrosted. Serve on the side.

Notes:

1. We used 1 batch of our Freeze and save one-pot big-batch chicken in this recipe.

2. To defrost the chicken and the sauces, transfer them to the fridge the day before you need them. Always place cooked meat on a higher shelf than raw meat and vegetables. Alternately, you can use the defrost setting on a microwave.

3. For the broccoli: Cut a head of broccoli into florets. Cook in a saucepan of boiling water for 3-4 minutes or until tender-crisp. Drain and plunge into cold water to stop the cooking. Pat the broccoli with paper towel to dry. Place the broccoli in a singe layer on a tray. Place in the freezer for 1 hour or until partially frozen. Transfer to a freezer bag and store in the freezer. Microwave to serve.

Slow-cooker Paprika Chicken

 Servings: 4   Cooking Time: 4 Hours 15 Mins.

Ingredients:

- 1 1/2 tbsp olive oil
- 8 Coles RSPCA Approved Chicken Drumsticks
- 1 brown onion, chopped
- 2 rindless shortcut bacon rashers, finely chopped
- 1 large red capsicum, chopped
- 2 garlic cloves, finely chopped
- 2 tsp sweet paprika
- 2 tbsp plain flour
- 410g can crushed tomatoes
- 2 cups Massel chicken style liquid stock
- 1/2 cup medium-grain white rice
- 150g green beans, trimmed, cut into 3cm lengths
- 1 tbsp Bulla Light Sour Cream
- Chopped fresh flat-leaf parsley, to serve

Directions:

1. Heat 2 teaspoons oil in a large, deep non-stick frying pan. Cook chicken, in batches, until browned all over. Transfer to the bowl of a 5.5-litre slow cooker.

2. Heat remaining oil in pan. Add onion and bacon. Cook, stirring, for 5 minutes or until onion is softened. Add capsicum. Cook, stirring, for 2 minutes. Add garlic and paprika. Cook for 1 minute or until fragrant. Add flour. Stir to coat all over. Cook for 1 minute. Add tomato, then stock, stirring until well combined. Season with pepper. Carefully transfer to slow cooker.

3. Cover with lid. Cook on low for 3 hours.

4. Increase heat to high. Transfer chicken to plate. Add rice to slow cooker. Stir well to combine. Return chicken to slow cooker. Cook, covered, for 40 minutes or until rice is just tender.

5. Remove lid. Add beans. Cook for 15 minutes or until rice and beans are tender. Stir in sour cream. Stand for 5 minutes to allow sauce to thicken. Serve sprinkled with parsley.

Chicken Pesto Roll-ups

 Servings: 4

Ingredients:

- 4 boneless skinless chicken breast halves (6 ounces each)
- 1/2 cup prepared pesto, divided
- 1 pound medium fresh mushrooms, sliced
- 4 slices reduced-fat provolone cheese, halved

Directions:

1. Preheat oven to 350°. Pound chicken breasts with a meat mallet to 1/4-in. thickness. Spread 1/4 cup pesto over chicken breasts.

2. Coarsely chop half the sliced mushrooms; scatter remaining sliced mushrooms in a 15x10x1-in. baking pan coated with cooking spray. Top each chicken breast with a fourth of the chopped mushrooms and a halved cheese slice. Roll up chicken from a short side; secure with toothpicks. Place seam side down on top of the sliced mushrooms.

3. Bake, covered, until chicken is no longer pink, 25-30 minutes. Preheat broiler; top chicken with remaining pesto and remaining cheese. Broil until cheese is melted and browned, 3-5 minutes longer. Discard toothpicks.

Pot-roast Chicken With Stock

Servings: 4　　**Cooking Time:** 2 Hours 10 Mins.

Ingredients:

- 2 tbsp olive oil
- 2.4kg chicken – buy the best you can afford
- 4 onions, peeled and cut into large wedges
- ½ bunch thyme
- 3 garlic cloves
- 6 peppercorns
- 175ml white wine
- 1.2l chicken stock

Directions:

1. Heat oven to 170C/150C fan/gas 5. Heat the oil in a large flameproof casserole dish and brown the chicken well on all sides, then sit it breast-side up. Pack in the onions, thyme, garlic and peppercorns, pour over the wine and stock, and bring to the boil. Pop on the lid and transfer to the oven for 2 hrs.

2. Remove and rest for 20 mins. Carefully lift the chicken onto a chopping board and carve as much as you need. Serve the carved chicken in a shallow bowl with the onions and some of the stock poured over. Serve with some usual Sunday veg and roast potatoes.

3. Strain the leftover stock into a bowl and strip the carcass of all the chicken. Chill both for up to three days or freeze for up to a month to use for other recipes like our one-pot chicken noodle soup.

Slow Cooker Chicken And Mushroom Stroganoff

Servings: 4　　**Cooking Time:** 5 Hours

Ingredients:

- 4 boneless skinless chicken breasts cubed
- 8 ounce sliced mushrooms
- 1 8 ounce cream cheese softened
- 1 10 1/2 ounce cream of chicken soup
- 1 envelope 1 1/4 ounce dry onion soup mix
- salt and pepper to taste
- fresh parsley chopped for garnish
- 8 ounces large egg noodles for serving

Directions:

1. Place the chicken in the bottom of a lightly greased slow cooker. Then add the mushrooms on top.

2. In a medium-sized bowl add cream cheese, cream of chicken soup, and dry onion soup mix. Mix until incorporated and spread on top of chicken and mushrooms.

3. Cook on low for 4-6 hours or high for Serve over noodles and top with fresh parsley and salt and pepper.

Slow Cooker Chicken And Biscuit Casserole

👥 Servings: 6   🕐 Cooking Time: 3 Hours 5 Mins.

Ingredients:

- 1 rotisserie chicken meat picked off the bones and cubed (about 3 cups)
- 1 cup milk
- 21 oz. cream of chicken soup
- 1 tsp. onion powder
- 1 tsp. garlic powder
- 2 tsp. chili powder
- ½ tsp. ground black pepper
- 2 cups shredded sharp cheese divided
- 2 cups frozen mixed vegetables from a 10-16 oz. bag
- 16.3 oz. can refrigerated biscuit dough Pillsury works best

Directions:

1. Spray the oval slow cooker with nonstick spray. In a large bowl stir together the chicken, cream of chicken soup, milk, seasonings, 1/2 the cheese and all the frozen mixed vegetables. Cut each biscuit into 6 pieces each. Stir the biscuits into the soup mixture.
2. Pour that mixture into the slow cooker and sprinkle with the remaining cheese.
3. Cook on low for 5-4 hours or until the biscuits are set in the middle.

Notes:

1. Want to cook in the oven? Follow the directions for mixing and pour everything into a prepared baking dish. Place the baking dish into a preheated oven (no more than 375 degrees) and cook for 35-45 minutes uncovered until the biscuits are no longer doughy.
2. Extra cheese, a dollop of sour cream, chopped bacon, and chopped green onions make perfect toppings.
3. Add any remaining casserole into an airtight container and keep them in the fridge for up to 3 days. Reheat over medium heat to medium high heat.

Slow Cooker Honey Garlic Chicken

👥 Servings: 4   🕐 Cooking Time: 6 Hours

Ingredients:

- 800 g chicken thigh fillets
- 2 cm piece fresh root ginger, peeled and grated
- 5 garlic cloves, crushed
- 100 ml runny honey
- 75 ml dark soy sauce
- 50 ml oyster sauce
- 1 tbsp. Sriracha hot sauce
- 2 tbsp. cornflour
- 1 tbsp. sesame seeds, toasted (optional)
- 4 spring onions, sliced (optional)

Directions:

1. Put the chicken, ginger, garlic, honey, soy, oyster sauce and Sriracha into the bowl of the slow cooker and mix. Cover and cook on low for 6hr, until the chicken is cooked through and tender.
2. Remove chicken with a slotted spoon to a chopping board. Pour the cooking liquid into a medium pan. In a small bowl, mix the cornflour with 2tbsp of the cooking liquid to form a thick paste. Add the cornflour paste to the pan and simmer over medium-high heat for 2min until thickened, whisking continuously.
3. Chop the chicken into bite-size pieces, stir into the thickened sauce and cook just until heated through. Sprinkle over the sesame seeds and spring onions, if using, and serve with rice and broccoli if you like.

Slow Cooker Thai Chicken Curry

 Servings: 4   Cooking Time: 6-8 Hours

Ingredients:

- 3 tbsp Thai green curry paste
- 400ml coconut milk
- 800g skinless and boneless chicken thighs, halved
- 1 aubergine, chopped
- 2 fresh lemongrass stalks, sliced
- thumbsized piece root ginger, sliced
- 6 lime leaves
- 1 tbsp brown sugar
- 1 tbsp fish sauce
- To serve
- cooked rice and fresh Thai basil leaves

Directions:

1. Gently fry the Thai green curry paste in a dry non-stick frying pan until fragrant, then pour in the coconut milk. Mix well until smooth then take off the heat.
2. Put the chicken thighs into a slow cooker along with the aubergine, lemongrass stalks, sliced ginger, lime leaves, brown sugar and fish sauce.
3. Pour over the curried coconut milk, give everything a good stir with a wooden spoon then cook on low for 6-8 hours.
4. Serve with rice and Thai basil scattered over.

Slow Cooker Chicken Chili

Servings: 6-8   Cooking Time: 6 Hours

Ingredients:

- 2 pounds ground chicken, coarsely ground preferred
- 3 tablespoons chili powder, plus 2 teaspoons
- 1 (15-ounce) can kidney beans, drained and rinsed
- 1 (15-ounce) can white beans, drained and rinsed
- 2 (28-ounce) cans diced fire roasted tomatoes
- 1 medium sweet potato (about 10 ounces), peeled and shredded
- 1 (15-ounce) can low-sodium chicken broth
- 1/4 cup instant tapioca (recommended: Minute tapioca)
- 1 to 2 chipotle chiles in adobo sauce with seeds, chopped
- 2 tablespoons soy sauce
- 1 tablespoon kosher salt
- 1 tablespoon onion powder
- 2 teaspoons granulated garlic
- 1 teaspoon dried oregano
- 1 teaspoon ground cumin
- 1/4 teaspoon ground cinnamon
- Pinch ground cloves
- 1/2 to 3/4 cup lager-style beer, optional
- Toppings: Sour cream, shredded Cheddar or Jack cheese, chopped scallions, and chopped pickled jalapenos

Directions:

1. Put the chicken in the slow cooker. Add 3 tablespoons of the chili powder and all the rest of the ingredients, except the beer. Stir everything together, cover, and cook on LOW for 6 to 8 hours.
2. Just before serving, stir in the remaining 2 teaspoons of chili powder, the beer, if using, and season with more salt and pepper, to taste, if desired. Divide the chili among warm bowls. Serve with the topping of your choice.
3. Know-How: Stirring in chili powder right before serving brightens the flavor of the chili.

Slow Cooker Whole Chicken

👥 Servings: 6   🕐 Cooking Time: 8 Hours

Ingredients:

- 5 lb. small whole chicken (look for a chicken that is on the smaller size around 4-5 lbs.)
- 1/2 cup butter
- 1 lemon (optional)
- 4 carrots peeled and halved
- 1 red onion peeled and quartered
- 1/2 tsp. dried thyme (rosemary or oregano can be substituted)
- 1 tsp. salt
- 1/2 tsp. paprika
- 1/4 tsp. garlic powder
- 1/4 tsp. pepper

Directions:

1. Add the carrots and onion to the bottom of the slow cooker.
2. Remove the chicken from its packaging. Remove any extra parts or packaging from the inside of the chicken. Drain off any liquid from the inside of the chicken.
3. Add the chicken on top of the vegetables.
4. Pour over the melted butter over the chicken.
5. Cut the lemon in half and squeeze over the chicken.
6. Sprinkle over the seasonings evenly.
7. Place the lid on the slow cooker.
8. Cook on LOW for 7-8 hours. This can vary for each chicken you cook, for they can vary in size. You know the chicken is done cooking when the drumsticks start pulling away from the breasts and the juices run clear. If you are concerned if your chicken is done, use a thermometer. 165° Fahrenheit is the safe temperature for chicken.

Notes:

1. Should I add water?
2. There is no need to add water to a whole chicken recipe in the slow cooker.
3. Adding butter or lemon juice is better for infusing flavor. Unless you want poached chicken, do not add water. Adding water can make your whole chicken taste bland.
4. What instead can I use to raise the chicken out of the cooking liquid?
5. The reason we place something like carrots and onion under the chicken is to keep it out of the cooking liquid so it doesn't turn into a soup. Try one of these methods if you prefer something other than carrots and onion.
6. Foil balls - You can take sheets of foil and ball them up. About 5 works well.
7. Small metal rack (such as the rack included in an instant pot)
8. Potatoes - Quartered potatoes also work well.
9. Does the slow cooker brown or crisp the chicken?
10. No, the slow cooker can not brown food for there is no browning element.
11. I use paprika to give a browned look for my whole chicken recipes.
12. You can put your slow cooked chicken under a broiler in an oven if you want crispy skin. Be sure your slow cooker is rated for such high temperature first, or place the chicken on a sheet pan.

Slow-cooked Coq Au Vin

Servings: 4   **Cooking Time:** 8 Hours 30 Mins.

Ingredients:

- 1.6kg whole chicken or 4 chicken marylands
- 200g speck, cut into small strips
- 2 garlic cloves, crushed
- 60ml (1/4 cup) brandy
- 35g (1/4 cup) plain flour
- 500ml (2 cups) Massel chicken style liquid stock
- 100g butter, chopped
- 8 French shallots
- 1 tbsp caster sugar
- 125ml (1/2 cup) water
- 2 tbsp olive oil
- 300g button mushrooms, trimmed
- 2 tbsp chopped fresh continental parsley
- Fresh thyme sprigs, to serve
- Crusty bread rolls or baguette, to serve
- Marinade
- 750ml (3 cups) pinot noir
- 2 carrots, thickly sliced
- 2 celery sticks, trimmed, thickly sliced
- 1 brown onion, cut into wedges
- 3 garlic cloves, crushed
- 3 French shallots, peeled, halved
- 2 tsp black peppercorns
- 2 dried bay leaves
- 10 sprigs fresh thyme
- 1 tsp salt

Directions:

1. To make marinade, place all ingredients in a large saucepan over medium-high heat and bring to the boil. Set aside to cool and allow the flavours to infuse.

2. Meanwhile, to joint the chicken, use a sharp knife or poultry shears to cut down either side of the backbone. Discard the bone. Halve the chicken through the breastbone. With chicken skin-side up, cut in half between the thigh and breast. Trim wings at first joint and discard bones.

3. Place chicken and the marinade in a bowl. Cover with plastic wrap and place in the fridge for 3 hours to marinate.

4. Remove chicken from marinade and pat dry with paper towel. Strain marinade into a bowl. Reserve vegetable mixture.

5. Heat a large frying pan over medium heat. Add the speck and cook, stirring occasionally, for 3 minutes or until the fat renders (releases from speck and melts) and the speck is golden. Remove speck with a slotted spoon and drain on paper towel. Return the frying pan to medium-high heat. Add chicken and brown, in 2 batches, for 3 minutes each side. Transfer to a bowl. Drain all but 2 tbs fat from the dish, then return to heat. Add the garlic and reserved vegetable mixture and cook, stirring occasionally, for 6 minutes or until vegetables are soft. Add brandy and use a long match to carefully ignite. Allow the flame to burn out, then stir in flour. Gradually stir in the stock, then reserved marinade. Place mixture in a slow cooker and top with chicken. Cover and cook on low for 6-8 hours or until chicken is tender and almost falling off the bone.

6. Meanwhile, melt half the butter in a large saucepan over medium-high heat. Add shallots and sugar, and cook, stirring occasionally, for 5 minutes or until shallots caramelise. Add water and bring to boil. Simmer for 8 minutes or until syrupy.

7. Heat oil and remaining butter in a frying pan over high heat. Add mushrooms and toss for 5 minutes or until golden. Season.

8. Add the speck, eschalot mixture and mushrooms to slow cooker. Cover and cook for 30 minutes to heat through. Season. Scatter with parsley and thyme sprigs. Serve with the bread.

Hainanese Chicken Rice

Servings: 4 **Cooking Time: 6 Hours 15 Mins.**

Ingredients:

- 1.2kg Coles RSPCA approved whole chicken
- 1 tbsp light soy sauce
- 1 tbsp mirin
- 4cm-piece fresh ginger, peeled, thickly sliced
- 4 spring onions, ends trimmed
- 2 tsp peanut oil
- 2 garlic cloves, finely chopped
- 1 tbsp fresh ginger, finely grated, extra
- 1 1/2 cups (300g) long-grain white rice, rinsed, drained
- 2 Lebanese cucumbers, thinly sliced lengthways
- Coriander leaves, to serve
- Soy sauce, extra (optional), to serve

- Chilli sauce
- 2 long red chillies, seeded, finely chopped
- 1 garlic clove, finely chopped
- 1/2 tsp salt
- 2 tsp fresh ginger, finely grated
- 1 tbsp lime juice
- 2 tsp light soy sauce
- Spring onion sauce
- 4 spring onions, ends trimmed, thinly sliced
- 1 tbsp finely grated fresh ginger
- 1/4 cup (60ml) peanut oil
- 1 tsp sesame oil
- 1 tbsp mirin

Directions:

1. Pat the chicken cavity dry with paper towel. Combine the soy sauce and mirin in a small bowl. Brush inside the chicken cavity. Place the sliced ginger and spring onion in the cavity. Place the chicken, breast-side down, in a slow cooker. Pour in enough cold water to cover the chicken completely. Cook on low for 6 hours or until the chicken is cooked through. Reserve the poaching liquid.

2. Meanwhile, to make the chilli sauce, place the chilli, garlic and salt in a mortar and gently pound with a pestle until a paste forms. Add the ginger, lime juice and soy sauce and stir to combine.

3. Heat the 2 teaspoon of peanut oil in a large saucepan over medium heat. Add the garlic and grated ginger. Cook, stirring, for 1 min or until fragrant. Stir in the rice. Add 2 cups (500ml) of reserved poaching liquid and bring to the boil. Reduce heat to low and cook, covered, for 11 mins or until liquid is absorbed and rice is tender. Set aside, covered, for 5 mins to rest.

4. To make the spring onion sauce, combine the spring onion and ginger in a small heatproof bowl. Combine the peanut oil and sesame oil in a small saucepan over high heat. Heat until very hot. Carefully pour the hot oil over the onion mixture. Stir in the mirin.

5. Cut chicken into portions, or discard bones and coarsely shred, if desired. Arrange on a serving platter with the cucumber and coriander. Serve with the rice, chilli sauce, spring onion sauce and extra soy sauce, if desired.

Notes:

1. On the stovetop:
2. If you don't have a slow cooker, poach the chicken in a stockpot or large heavy-based saucepan over very low heat for 1 hour or until cooked through

Slow Cooker Moroccan Chicken

👪 Servings: 6   🕐 Cooking Time: 3 Hours 35 Mins.

Ingredients:

- 1 tbsp extra virgin olive oil
- 1 large red onion, cut into wedges
- 2 garlic cloves, crushed
- 2 tsp ground cumin
- 2 tsp ground coriander
- 2 tsp ground cinnamon
- 2 tsp smoked paprika
- 1/2 tsp ground turmeric
- 1 salt-reduced chicken stock pot
- 2 carrots, thickly sliced
- 1 large red capsicum, thickly sliced
- 1 large zucchini, halved lengthways, thickly sliced
- 6 skinless chicken thigh cutlets
- 400g can cherry tomatoes in juice
- 1/2 lemon, thinly sliced
- 2 tbsp Coles Pure Australian Honey
- 1/2 cup pitted green olives
- 1/2 cup fresh coriander sprigs
- Cooked couscous, to serve
- Lemon wedges, to serve

Directions:

1. Heat oil in flameproof slow cooker bowl or a frying pan over medium-high heat. Add onion. Cook, stirring, for 3 minutes or until charred. Add garlic and spices. Cook, stirring, for 1 minute or until fragrant.

2. Transfer bowl to slow cooker. Add stock, carrot, capsicum and zucchini. Place chicken on vegetables. Pour over tomatoes. Top with lemon slices and drizzle with honey. Season with salt and pepper. Cover. Cook on HIGH for 3 hours (or LOW for 6 hours). Add olives. Cook on HIGH for 30 minutes or until chicken is cooked through.

3. Sprinkle with coriander sprigs. Serve with couscous and extra lemon wedges.

Slow Cooker Chicken Chasseur

👪 Servings: 4   🕐 Cooking Time: 6 Hours 20 Mins.

Ingredients:

- 2 tsp. vegetable oil
- 8 bone-in skin-on chicken thighs
- 1 onion, finely chopped
- 200 g bacon lardons
- 1 garlic clove, crushed
- 2 tbsp. tomato purée
- 150 ml dry white wine
- 200 ml hot chicken stock
- 200 g button mushrooms
- 400 g tin chopped tomatoes
- Small handful tarragon leaves, finely chopped, to serve

Directions:

1. Heat oil in a large frying pan over medium heat. Add chicken to the pan and brown all over, in batches if necessary. Remove to the bowl of a slow cooker.

2. Add onion and bacon to the pan and cook, stirring, until onion is softened, about 10min. Add garlic and tomato purée and cook for 2min. Increase heat to medium-high and stir in the wine. Bubble to reduce wine by 1/

3. Transfer mixture to the slow cooker. Add the stock, mushrooms, tomatoes and some seasoning. Stir. Cover and cook on low for 6hr.

4. Divide between 4 plates and sprinkle over the tarragon. Serve with mashed potato and seasonal greens, if you like.

Slow-cooked Chicken Caesar Wraps

Servings: 6   **Cooking Time: 3 Hours**

Ingredients:

- 1-1/2 pounds boneless skinless chicken breast halves
- 2 cups chicken broth
- 3/4 cup creamy Caesar salad dressing
- 1/2 cup shredded Parmesan cheese
- 1/4 cup minced fresh parsley
- 1/2 teaspoon pepper
- 6 flour tortillas (8 inches)
- 2 cups shredded lettuce
- Optional: Salad croutons, crumbled cooked bacon and additional shredded Parmesan cheese

Directions:

1. Place chicken and broth in a 1-1/2- or 3-qt. slow cooker. Cook, covered, on low 3-4 hours or until a thermometer inserted in chicken reads 165°. Remove chicken and discard cooking juices. Shred chicken with 2 forks; return to slow cooker.

2. Stir in dressing, Parmesan, parsley and pepper; heat through. Serve in tortillas with lettuce and, if desired, salad croutons, crumbled bacon and additional shredded Parmesan cheese.

Slow Cooker Salsa Chicken

Servings: 4   **Cooking Time: 4 Hours 15 Mins.**

Ingredients:

- 2 pounds chicken breasts boneless, skinless (about 4)
- 2 cups salsa mild
- 1 cup Mexican Blend cheese shredded

Directions:

1. Prepare chicken: Place whole chicken breasts in your Slow Cooker then pour the salsa over each breast.

2. Cook: Cook anywhere from 1 1/2 to 2 hours on high or 4 hours on low, you don't want to cook it longer because it will start falling apart.

3. Preheat your oven to 425 F degrees.

4. Add Cheese: Transfer the chicken to a 9x13 inch baking dish. Spoon some of the leftover salsa over the chicken. Sprinkle each breast with cheese, about 1/4 cup of cheese for each breast.

5. Bake: Place the baking dish in the oven and bake for 15 minutes or until the cheese is golden brown and is bubbling.

Notes:

1. It's not really recommended to cook frozen chicken in the slow cooker as there's risk of bacteria contaminating the meat before it reaches a safe temperature. I would thaw it out in the microwave first for a few minutes before actually adding it to the slow cooker.

2. Please keep in mind that nutritional information is a rough estimate and can vary greatly based on products used.

Slow Cooker Chicken Breast

Servings: 8   **Cooking Time: 4 Hours**

Ingredients:

- 2 lbs. boneless skinless chicken breast
- ½ tsp. salt
- ½ tsp. garlic powder
- ½ tsp. onion powder
- ¼ tsp. pepper
- ¾ cup low sodium chicken broth

Directions:

1. Season your chicken breast with salt, garlic powder, onion powder, and pepper.
2. Place your chicken in your Slow Cooker and cover them with the chicken broth.
3. Cook on low for 4 hours, or until the chicken reaches 165 degrees. The chicken should be cooked through, and will be sliceable.
4. You can cook it past this point, though, it will shred instead of slice. If you want shredded chicken, you can cook for up to 8 hours.
5. Let the chicken rest on a cutting board for 10 minutes before slicing (covered lightly with foil). Slice and serve OR place in fridge and slice later in the week when you need it.
6. Strain your chicken broth using a sieve and remove all of the bits of chicken and fat. Take the strained chicken broth and use in your recipes right away or freeze.

Notes:

1. This recipe is specifically to use the chicken breast into other dishes, so the seasonings are very simple. Additional seasoning that can pair with lots of meals, is paprika, and thyme.
2. Keep the breasts whole until you are ready to use them. Slice it just before adding it to your desired recipe. The chicken will stay moister and taste fresher if you slice as needed.
3. Cooked chicken is good in the refrigerator for 3-4 days. Or in the freezer for 2 months.

Slow Cooker Cajun Chicken Fettuccine

Servings: 8   **Cooking Time: 6 Hours**

Ingredients:

- 1 cup chicken broth
- 1/4 tsp. cayenne pepper
- 1/2 tsp. garlic powder
- 1/4 tsp. onion powder
- 1/2 tsp. dried leaf oregano
- 1/4 tsp. red pepper flakes
- 1 1/2 tsp. paprika
- 1 tsp. salt
- 1/4 tsp. pepper

- 2 lbs. boneless skinless chicken breasts
- 1 small white onion diced
- Add at the end:
- 1 lb. fettuccine noodles cooked according to package Directions:
- 2 cups heavy cream
- 3/4 cup parmesan cheese divided
- dried parsley or oregano for garnish
- paprika for garnish

Directions:

1. Add the chicken broth to the slow cooker, add the cayenne, garlic powder, onion powder, oregano, red pepper flakes, paprika, salt and pepper. Stir.

2. Add the chicken breasts and flip them around in the seasoned chicken broth to get the seasonings on the chicken.

3. Sprinkle the onions over the chicken and broth.

4. Cover and cook on low for 6 hours without opening the lid during the cooking time.

5. After the cooking time is done, shred the chicken with two forks right in the slow cooker. Add the heavy cream.

6. Add the cooked and drained pasta and a ½ cup of the Parmesan cheese. Stir.

7. Sprinkle over the remaining parmesan cheese. I added a touch more paprika and also parsley flakes to the top of my pasta to make it look pretty. Cover and cook for 20 more minutes. Cooking for a bit longer helps the sauce thicken from the gluten in the pasta.

8. Serve and enjoy!

Notes:

1. To make this a complete meal stir in steamed veggies into the pasta with the noodles at the end of the cooking time.

2. You can add a block of cream cheese to this dish instead of heavy cream. You can add it at the beginning of the cooking time or microwave it for 30 seconds before adding the dish at the end of the cooking time.

3. Cayenne pepper loses its potency the longer it's been on the shelf or it can sometimes not be as spicy as other brands. You can add additional cayenne pepper after the dish is done cooking to taste.

4. You can use two teaspoons of cajun spice seasoning (such as Tony's Chachere's Creole Seasoning) instead of the different seasonings in this dish. Don't add any more, for it can be on the salty side.

Slow Cooker Teriyaki Chicken

👥 Servings: 6   🕐 Cooking Time: 6 Hours

Ingredients:

- ½ cup soy sauce
- ½ cup mirin see notes for substitutes
- ½ cup rice wine vinegar
- ½ cup brown sugar
- ¼ cup cornstarch
- 1 Tbsp. fresh ginger grated
- 1 Tbsp. fresh garlic grated
- 1 Tbsp. toasted sesame seeds plus more for garnish
- 2 lbs. chicken breasts
- green onions sliced for garnish

Directions:

1. In a medium sized bowl, whisk together the soy sauce, mirin, rice wine vinegar, brown sugar, cornstarch, ginger, garlic and sesame seeds.
2. Add the chicken breast to the bottom of the slow cooker in a single layer, pour over the soy sauce mixture.
3. Cook on HIGH for 3 hours or LOW for 5-6 hours or until tender and shreddable and the sauce has thickened.
4. Remove the chicken from the slow cooker to a medium sized bowl and shred using two forks into larger pieces. Stir the chicken back into the sauce.
5. Serve over rice and garnish with toasted sesame seeds and sliced scallions. Enjoy!

Notes:

1. When grating fresh garlic cloves, you do not need to peel it as it peels itself when grating and wont go through the grater.
2. When grating fresh ginger, you do not need to peel it as skin will be grated into small pieces. Wash the fresh ginger root thoroughly with cold water before grating.
3. Store leftovers in an airtight container for up to 3 days in the refrigerator.
4. Reheat portions in the microwave.
5. If you do not have or can't get mirin, it can be substituted with unfiltered sake, dry sherry or sweet marsala wine.
6. Chicken thighs can be used in place of chicken breast. Chicken thighs tend to cook a little faster then chicken breast so the cooking times may vary.

Slow Cooker Asian Chicken Lettuce Wraps

👥 Servings: 6   🕐 Cooking Time: 3 Hours

Ingredients:

- 2 lbs ground chicken (not ground chicken breast)
- 3 cloves garlic , minced
- 1 red bell pepper , cored and finely chopped
- 1/2 cup finely chopped yellow onion
- 1/2 cup hoisin sauce
- 2 Tbsp soy sauce
- Salt and freshly ground black pepper
- 1 (8 oz) can sliced water chestnuts, drained and rinsed
- 1 1/2 cups cooked white or brown rice
- 3 green onions , sliced
- 1 Tbsp rice vinegar and 1 1/2 tsp sesame oil (optional)
- 2 heads iceberg lettuce

Directions:

1. Place ground chicken and garlic in a large microwave safe bowl. Microwave mixture, stirring occasionally, until chicken is no longer pink, about 5 - 6 minutes. Drain off liquid and pour mixture into a 5 - 7 quart slow cooker.

2. Add bell pepper, onion, hoisin sauce, soy sauce, 1/2 tsp salt and 1/2 tsp pepper and toss mixture. Cover and cook on low heat 2 - 3 hours until chicken is tender.

3. Stir in water chestnuts, cooked rice, green onions, rice vinegar, and sesame oil, cook until heated through 3 - 5 minutes. Season with additional salt as desired. Separate iceberg lettuce leaves and serve with chicken filling.

Slow Cooker Turkey

👥 Servings: 2   🕐 Cooking Time: 3-4 Hours

Ingredients:

- 2 turkey breasts, skinless
- 1 medium carrot, chopped
- 1 onion, peeled and quartered
- 6 peppercorns
- 1 bay leaf
- 1 rosemary sprig
- few thyme sprigs
- 125ml white wine (optional)
- roast potatoes, carrots and greens, to serve

Directions:

1. Season the turkey all over and put in the slow cooker with all the remaining ingredients, along with 1 litre of water. Set your slow cooker to low and cook for 3-4 hrs until no pink meat remains, or a meat thermometer reads 75C at the thickest part of the breast.

2. Remove the turkey from the slow cooker and serve, or cover with foil and leave to rest while you make gravy using the stock that remains. Serve the turkey with the gravy, roast potatoes, carrots and greens.

Notes:

1. This recipe works for a turkey crown but you'll need to cook on high for 3-5 hrs depending on the size of the turkey. If you have a meat thermometer, the thickest part should reach 75C.

Slow Cooker Summer Chicken Casserole

 Servings: 4   Cooking Time: 6 Hours 25 Mins.

Ingredients:

- 2 garlic cloves, crushed
- 1 tsp. dried chilli flakes
- 8 bone-in skin-on chicken thighs
- 1 tsp. olive oil
- 3 x 400g tins butter beans, drained and rinsed
- 750 ml hot chicken stock
- 400 g Tenderstem broccoli
- Finely grated zest 1 lemon
- 25 g flat-leaf parsley, leaves picked and roughly chopped

Directions:

1. In a large bowl, mix the garlic, chilli flakes and some seasoning. Add the chicken and toss to coat.
2. Heat oil in a large non-stick frying pan over medium-high heat. Fry chicken until browned all over, in batches if necessary. Remove to a plate.
3. Put the butter beans and stock in the bowl of a slow cooker. Stir gently. Arrange the chicken on top and cover with the lid. Cook on low for 6hr, or until the chicken is cooked through and falling off the bone.
4. Add the broccoli, pushing it down into the beans and stock to make sure it's covered. Re-cover with the lid and cook for a further 15min. 5 Stir through the lemon zest and parsley, check seasoning and serve.

Slow Cooker Green Chile Chicken And Rice Casserole

 Servings: 8   Cooking Time: 8 Hours

Ingredients:

- 1 1/2 lbs boneless skinless chicken breasts
- 1/2 tsp. salt
- 1/4 tsp. pepper
- 2 tsp. chili powder
- 1/2 tsp. garlic powder
- 1/2 tsp. onion powder
- 1 small white onion, diced
- 1 poblano pepper, diced (about 1/2 cup)
- 19 oz. can green enchilada sauce
- Add these ingredients at the end:
- 1 cup sour cream
- 2 cups shredded cheddar cheese, divided
- 1/4 cup sliced green onion
- 3 cups hot cooked white rice

Directions:

1. Add the chicken breasts to the slow cooker. Sprinkle over the salt, pepper, garlic powder, onion powder and chili powder over the chicken. Add the onion, poblano pepper. Pour over the enchilada sauce.
2. Cover and cook for 6-8 hours on the low setting.
3. When the cooking time is done, shred the chicken with two forks. Add the sour cream, half cup of the cheese and the green onion. Stir. Add the cooked rice and stir. Sprinkle over the remaining cheese.
4. Place the lid back on and cook for 15 more minutes or until the cheese is melted. If your rice has cooled and not hot, you will need to cook longer about 45 minutes on high.

MEAT RECIPES

Slow-cooked Celeriac With Pork & Orange

 Servings: 6

Ingredients:

- 3 leeks, trimmed and washed
- 2 carrots, peeled
- 3 tbsp olive oil
- 900g boneless pork, cut into large stewing pieces (shoulder is an ideal cut to use)
- 2 small or 1 large celeriac (about 1kg/2lb 4oz), peeled and diced into large chunks
- 2 garlic cloves, chopped
- 200ml dry white wine
- 200ml chicken stock
- juice and zest of 1 orange (remove the orange zest with a potato peeler)
- 2 tsp soy sauce
- large sprig of rosemary
- crusty bread, to serve

Directions:

1. Preheat the oven to fan 120C/conventional 140C/gas Cut each leek into about five pieces, chop the carrots into pieces the same size as the leeks. Heat a large, lidded, flameproof casserole dish on the hob until it's very hot. Add 2 tbsp of the olive oil, then carefully tip the pork into the casserole and leave it for a couple of minutes to brown. Stir once, then leave for another couple of minutes. Using a slotted spoon, transfer the meat to a plate. Pour the rest of the oil into the dish, tip in the leeks, carrots and celeriac and fry for 3-4 minutes, stirring, until they start to brown. Add the garlic and fry for a minute more.

2. Stir the pork and any juices into the vegetables, then pour in the wine, stock, orange juice and soy sauce. Throw in the rosemary and orange zest, season with salt and pepper, give it a stir, then bring everything to the boil.

3. Cover the dish, transfer it to the oven and cook for 2 hours, stirring after an hour. Cook until the pork is very tender and the leeks fall apart when prodded with a spoon. (It can now be left to cool and then frozen for up to 1 month.) Leave to stand for at least 10 minutes, then spoon into bowls. Serve with crusty bread to soak up all those juices.

Slow Cooker Meatball Subs Recipe

 Servings: 8

Ingredients:

- 32 oz. package frozen meatballs
- 48 oz. marinara sauce (two 24-oz. jars)
- 2 tsp. Italian seasoning
- 1 tsp. garlic powder
- For the subs:
- split hoagie rolls
- sliced provolone or shredded mozzarella cheese

Directions:

1. Prepare the slow cooker with nonstick cooking spray.
2. Add the sauce to the slow cooker and add garlic powder and Italian seasonings. Stir.
3. Add the meatballs to the slow cooker and stir.
4. Cook on HIGH for 3 hours or LOW for 5 hours. Stir occasionally to avoid burning around the edges.
5. Serve the meatballs on split hoagie rolls along with your favorite cheese.
6. PRO tip: Place the cheese down first, so your buns don't get soggy.

Notes:

1. Variations:
2. Sliders: In this recipe, we suggest putting the meatballs on hoagie buns or hoagie rolls, instead use small slider buns and use only one meatball per bun. Top it with additional sauce and sliced provolone or shredded mozzarella cheese.
3. Pizza Subs: Add a pepperoni on top of each meatball for a pizza-flavored sub. Also, top with red onion and olives.
4. Appetizer: Leaving the meatballs as-is will give you a good appetizer choice. Consider serving with a side of toothpicks and small squares of cheese.
5. Casserole: With the meatballs already made, you could easily use them for a cheesy casserole. Cook them in the Slow Cooker according to the directions below and top them with cheese. Serve with pasta and a side of garlic bread or garlic sticks.
6. Can I double this recipe?
7. Yes! If you're cooking for a larger crowd, simply double the amount of ingredients needed. Keep in mind the more you add, the longer it may take to cook.
8. How many meatballs should I serve per person?
9. Account for 4-5 meatballs per person when preparing it. Note you can double it if needed.

Slow-roast Rolled Pork Belly

👥 Servings: 6   🕐 Cooking Time: 3 Hours

Ingredients:

- 2 tbsp fennel seeds
- 1 tsp black peppercorns
- 3 garlic cloves , finely chopped
- 1 large bunch of fresh thyme, leaves only
- 3 tbsp olive oil
- 1.5 - 2kg 3lb 5oz - 4lb 8oz piece pork belly (skin on) cut from the slimmer half, skin scored
- 2 lemons

Directions:

1. Toast the spices in a dry frying pan for a couple of mins. Pound them together in a pestle and mortar with some flaked sea salt, the garlic and half the thyme to make a paste, then mix with 2 tbsp olive oil.

2. Lay the pork on a board skin-side down. Rub the herb mix all over the flesh then scatter with the remaining whole thyme leaves. Neatly roll the meat into a joint surrounded by the skin then use butchers' string to tie the joint tightly at regular intervals to hold the joint together. Cover and chill, leaving to marinate for a few hours or overnight.

3. When ready to cook, rub the skin of the joint with plenty of salt and 1 tbsp remaining olive oil. Put it on a wire rack and roast at 200C/180C fan/gas 6 for 30 mins. After this time, squeeze the lemons over the skin and turn the heat down to 180C/160C fan/gas 4. Roast for a further 2 hrs. Finally turn the heat back up to 220C/200C fan/gas 7 and give it a final blast for another 30 mins or so, to finish the crisping of the skin. Allow to rest somewhere warm for 20 mins. Carve up into thick slices and serve with your favourite roast dinner accompaniments.

Slow-cooker Beef Tacos

👥 Servings: 8

Ingredients:

- 1 small beef chuck roast (about 3 to 4 lbs.)
- 1 large onion, diced
- 4 cloves garlic, chopped
- Juice of 3 limes
- 1 tbsp. chili powder
- 1 tbsp. ground cumin
- 1 tbsp. dried oregano
- 4 c. low-sodium chicken broth
- 20 small corn tortillas
- Sour cream, green onions, red onion, and lime wedges for serving

Directions:

1. In a 5-quart slow-cooker, combine chuck roast, onion, garlic, lime juice, chili powder, cumin, and oregano, then pour over chicken broth. Cover and let cook on low, 8 hours.

2. When ready to shred, add roast and onion to a large bowl and shred with two forks. Pour over enough juice so it's nicely marinated.

3. Char tortillas over the flame of a gas burner, then top with beef and serve with sour cream, green onions, chopped red onion, and limes.

Slow-cooker Sausage Casserole

 Servings: 4   🕐 Cooking Time: 4 Hours.

Ingredients:

- 2 red onions, finely chopped
- 1 celery stick, finely chopped
- 1-2 tbsp rapeseed oil
- 4 carrots, cut into fat pieces
- 12 chipolatas, each halved
- 1 sweet potato, peeled and cut into chunks
- 400g tin tomatoes
- 1 tbsp tomato purée or tomato and veg purée
- 1 thyme sprig
- 1 rosemary sprig
- 1 beef stock cube or stock pot

Directions:

1. Fry the onion and celery in the oil over a low heat until it starts to soften and cook, about 5 mins, then spoon it into the slow cooker. Fry the carrots briefly and add them too.

2. Brown the sausages all over in the same frying pan – make sure they get a really good colour because they won't get any browner in the slow cooker. Transfer to the slow cooker and add the sweet potato and tomatoes.

3. Put the purée in the frying pan and add 250ml boiling water, swirl everything around to pick up every last bit of flavour, and tip the lot into the slow cooker. Add the herbs, stock cube and some pepper. Don't add salt until the casserole is cooked as the stock can be quite salty. Cook on high for 4 hrs or on low for 8 hrs, then serve or leave to cool and freeze.

Notes:

1. Slow cookers vary in capacity and efficiency – you may want to check casserole timings against the manufacturers' instructions on yours.

Slow-cooker Hawaiian Barbecue Ribs

 Servings: 4

Ingredients:

- 2 small racks baby back ribs (1 1/2 to 2 pounds each), cut in half
- Kosher salt and freshly ground pepper
- 2 tablespoons vegetable oil
- 3 tablespoons ancho chile powder
- 2/3 cup teriyaki-style barbecue sauce
- 1/3 cup apple cider vinegar
- 1 tablespoon grated peeled fresh ginger
- 2 cloves garlic, grated
- 1/4 cup pineapple preserves
- 2 tablespoons ketchup
- 2 scallions, thinly sliced on an angle

Directions:

1. Generously season the ribs with salt and pepper, then rub with the vegetable oil and sprinkle with the chile powder, pressing to adhere. Whisk 1/3 cup barbecue sauce, the vinegar, ginger and garlic in a 6- to 8-quart slow cooker. Add the ribs and turn to coat in the sauce. Cover and cook on low until the ribs are tender, 7 hours.

2. Preheat the broiler. Transfer the ribs to a rimmed baking sheet. Remove 1/4 cup of the cooking liquid to a small bowl and whisk in the remaining 1/3 cup barbecue sauce, the pineapple preserves and ketchup.

3. Brush the pineapple sauce all over the ribs to coat completely; arrange bone-side down. Broil until the sauce is sticky and the ribs are lightly charred in spots, 3 to 5 minutes. Top with the scallions.

Slow-roasted Pork Shoulder With Leeks, Apricots & Thyme

 Servings: 6-8 Cooking Time: 3 Hours

Ingredients:

- 2.5kg/5lb 8oz piece boned and rolled pork shoulder - free-range or rare breed is best
- 1 celery stick, cut into chunks
- 1 onion, thickly sliced
- 1 carrot, thickly sliced
- 150ml white wine or medium-dry cider
- 500ml strong-flavoured chicken or pork stock
- 1 tbsp plain flour
- 1 tbsp butter
- For the stuffing
- 25g butter
- 2 leeks, cleaned well and shredded
- 85g chopped dried apricot, soaked for 2 hrs in boiling water to cover, then drained
- 1 tsp chopped thyme leaf
- 140g fresh coarse breadcrumb

Directions:

1. A few hours before you want to cook the pork, remove it from the fridge and dry the skin thoroughly. Leave unwrapped in a cool place to slowly come to room temperature while you make the stuffing.

2. Put a large saucepan over a medium heat and add the butter. When it begins to sizzle, add the leeks and cook until they are soft and most of their liquid has evaporated. Stir in the apricots and thyme, season well and transfer to a bowl to cool. When the mixture is cold, stir in the breadcrumbs. Taste and season again if required.

3. When you are ready to cook the pork, heat oven to 220C/200C fan/gas 7. Spoon the stuffing into the pocket your butcher has left for you. Wipe any stuffing from the skin, put the pork in a roasting tin and season the skin well with salt. Put the celery, onion and carrot in the tin around the pork, place in the oven and cook for 30 mins.

4. Reduce heat to 140C/120C fan/ gas 1 and cook the pork for a further 2 hrs 30 mins. Transfer the pork to a warm serving dish to rest while you finish the gravy.

5. Tip out any fat from the roasting tin and reserve for another dish. Put the roasting tin on a medium heat, add the white wine or cider and, using a wooden spatula, scrape the caramelised juices from the bottom of the pan and allow them to dissolve. Let the juices reduce by half.

6. Add the stock and simmer for 5 mins. Add the flour and butter, mashed together, and whisk them into the gravy. Taste for seasoning, then strain into a warmed jug. If your pork skin has not crackled, put under a hot grill for a few mins, turning every 30 secs or so, until bubbled and crackling.

Slow-cooker Short Ribs

👪 Servings: 5

Ingredients:

- 2 tbsp. vegetable oil
- 5 lb. bone-in beef short ribs, cut crosswise into 2-inch pieces
- Kosher salt
- Freshly ground black pepper
- 1/2 c. low-sodium soy sauce
- 1/2 c. water
- 1/4 c. packed light brown sugar
- 1/4 c. rice vinegar
- 2 tsp. sesame oil
- 1 tsp. crush red pepper flakes (optional)
- 3 Carrots, medium, peeled and chopped into thirds
- 1 yellow onion, large, sliced into 1/2 inch wedges
- 5 cloves garlic, crushed
- 1 1/2 inch piece ginger, thinly sliced
- Toasted sesame seeds, for serving
- 2 green onions, thinly sliced, for serving
- Cooked short grain white rice, for serving

Directions:

1. Season short ribs with salt and pepper. Heat oil in a large Dutch oven over medium-high heat. Working in 2 batches, brown short ribs on all sides, about 8 minutes per batch. Transfer short ribs to slow cooker and pour off all but 3 tablespoons drippings from pot.

2. Meanwhile, whisk soy sauce, water, brown sugar, rice vinegar, sesame oil, and red pepper flakes.

3. Add carrots and onions to pan, and cook, mixing occasionally until browned. Add garlic and ginger and brown until fragrant, 1 minute more. Remove from heat and deglaze with reserved soy sauce mixture, scraping up any brown bits from the bottom. Pour this mixture into the slow cooker.

4. Cover slow cooker and cook on low for 9 to 10 hours, or on high for 4 to 5 hours, or until the meat is very tender and falling off the bone.

5. Garnish short ribs with toasted sesame seeds and green onions. Spoon sauce over rice and serve.

Slow Cooker Beer And Onion Beef Ribs

👥 Servings: 4   🕐 Cooking Time: 8 Hours.

Ingredients:

- 2 Tbsp. vegetable oil
- 4 lbs. beef back ribs (3-5 lbs. in total; I used 2 small packages; also called spare ribs)
- 1 oz. Lipton onion soup mix
- 1 large onion thickly sliced
- 12 oz. beer (I use Bud Light, Coors Light or any other light beer I have on hand)

Directions:

1. Place a large pan over medium-high heat. Coat the pan with cooking oil. Brown the beef ribs. (I could only brown one side since they have such a curve on the other side.) I left the ribs in 4-5 ribs per section, though you can cut the ribs individually if desired.
2. Place the ribs into a 6-quart slow cooker.
3. Add the onion soup mix, onions, and pour over the beer.
4. Cover and cook on LOW for 8 hours without opening the lid during the cooking time.
5. If you prefer, you can degrease the sauce before serving by placing paper towels over the top of the sauce and removing it! Works like a charm!

Notes:

1. You can use beef broth instead of beer if needed. You can also use a red wine such as red blend or merlot.
2. Place any leftover ribs into an airtight container and store them in the fridge for up to 4 days.
3. Want pork ribs instead? You can you country style ribs or pork baby back ribs.

Slow Cooker Pork Belly In Apricot Sauce

👥 Servings: 4   🕐 Cooking Time: 8 Hours

Ingredients:

- 1/2 cup apricot nectar
- 1/2 cup tomato sauce
- 1 tbsp Worcestershire sauce
- 2 tbsp sherry vinegar
- 1/4 cup dark brown sugar
- 2 tsp onion powder
- 1 tsp dried oregano
- 1 tsp cracked black pepper
- 1 tsp salt
- 1.4kg piece boneless pork belly
- Steamed lemon green beans, to serve
- Steamed halved asparagus, to serve

Directions:

1. Combine nectar, sauces, vinegar, sugar, onion powder, oregano, pepper and salt in a bowl.
2. Score pork rind in a diamond pattern (see note). Place half the sauce mixture in the bowl of a slow cooker. Add pork, rind-side down. Pour over remaining sauce. Cover. Cook on high for 3 hours (or low for 6 hours). Turn pork. Cook on high for a further 1 hour (or low for 2 hours) or until pork is tender.
3. Carefully transfer pork to a serving platter. Drizzle with some of the pan juices. Serve with steamed lemon green beans and asparagus.

Notes:

1. You'll need a 5 Litre slow cooker for this recipe.
2. Ask your butcher to score the pork rind for you.

Lamb Shanks In Red Wine Sauce

Servings: 4   **Cooking Time: 3 Hours 30 Mins.**

Ingredients:

- 4 lamb shanks , around 13 oz / 400g each
- 1 tsp EACH cooking/kosher salt and pepper
- 2 - 3 tbsp olive oil , separated
- 1 onion , finely diced (brown, yellow or white)
- 3 garlic cloves , minced
- 1 cup carrot , peeled, finely diced
- 1 cup celery , finely diced
- 2 1/2 cups red wine (full bodied
- 800 g / 28oz can crushed tomatoes

- 2 tbsp tomato paste
- 2 cups chicken stock , low sodium (or water)
- 5 sprigs of thyme (preferably tied together), or 2 tsp dried thyme
- 2 dried bay leaves (or 4 fresh)
- To Serve:
- Mashed potato , polenta or pureed cauliflower
- Fresh thyme leaves , optional garnish

Directions:

1. Preheat the oven to 180°C/350°F (all oven types - fan and standard).
2. Season shanks - Pat the lamb shanks dry and sprinkle with salt and pepper.
3. Brown - Heat 2 tablespoons of olive oil in a large heavy based pot over high heat. Sear the lamb shanks in 2 batches until brown all over, about 5 minutes. Remove lamb onto a plate and drain excess fat (if any) from the pot.
4. Sauté aromatics - Turn the heat down to medium low. Heat remaining 1 tablespoon of olive oil in the same pot. Add the onion and garlic, cook for 2 minutes. Add carrot and celery. Cook for 5 minutes until onion is translucent and sweet.
5. Braising liquid - Add the red wine, chicken stock, crushed tomato, tomato paste, thyme and bay leaves. Stir to combine.
6. Add shanks - Place the lamb shanks into the pot, squeezing them in to fit so they are mostly submerged.
7. Oven 2 hours covered - Turn stove up, bring liquid to a simmer. Cover, then transfer to the oven for 2 hours (see notes for other cook methods).
8. Uncovered 30 minutes - Remove lid, then return to the oven for another 30 minutes (so 2 1/2 hours in total). Check to ensure lamb meat is ultra tender - if not, cover and keep cooking. Ideal is tender meat but still just holding onto bone.
9. Remove lamb onto plate and keep warm. Pick out and discard bay leaves and thyme.
10. Sauce - Strain the sauce into a bowl, pressing to extract all sauce out of the veggies (Note 5 for repurposing the veggies). Pour strained sauce back into pot. If needed, bring to a simmer over medium heat and reduce slightly to a syrupy consistency - I rarely need to. Taste then add salt and pepper to taste
11. Serve the lamb shanks on mashed potato or cauliflower puree with plenty of sauce! Garnish with thyme leaves if desired.

Notes:

1. Lamb Shanks - sizes vary considerably so make sure you get ones that will fit in your cooking vessel! 4 x 400g/13oz lamb shanks fits snugly in a 26cm/11" diameter Chasseur dutch oven which is what I use. They don't need to be completely submerged, just as long as most of the meaty end is mostly submerged, that's fine. If you don't have a pot large enough, you can switch to a baking dish for the slow cooking part, and cover with a double layer of foil if you don't have a lid for it. You can also ask your butcher to cut the shaft so it bends if you are concerned, or to trim it slightly.
2. Cook time - 350-400g shanks should cook to "fall apart tender" but still holding onto bone in 2.5 hrs at 180°C/350°F. It can take up to 3 hrs, so to err on the side of caution re: dinner timing, give yourself 3 hours oven time. Shanks are the sort of thing that can sit around for ages and stay warm (keep covered in pot) and the flavour just gets even better. In fact, if you are cooking to impress, cook it the day before then reheat to serve - flavour will develop overnight, like with any stew!

3. Onion, carrot and celery is the "holy trinity" of slow cooking, creating a beautiful flavour base for the sauce. It's not a deal breaker to exclude the carrot and celery, but it does give the sauce an extra edge.
4. Wine - Use a good value full bodied red wine, like cabaret sauvignon or merlot. Shiraz is ok too. No need to use expensive wine for slow cooked recipes like this (and the New York Times agrees). Use discount end of bin specials (I get mine from Dan Murphey's). Pinots not suitable, too light. 99% of the alcohol in the red wine evaporates during cooking. The sauce does not taste winey at all, it completely transforms.
5. Non alcoholic sub: 1 1/2 cups beef broth LOW SODIUM, 1 cup water. + 1 tbsp Worcestershire Sauce. Beef has a stronger deeper flavour than chicken so will be more suited to being the sub for wine.
6. Most of the alcohol in the red wine will evaporate during this step but not completely - it will finish evaporating during the slow cooking. The sauce does not taste winey at all, it completely transforms.
7. Sauce options: The other option is to blitz the sauce using a sick blender. The sauce will be thicker, and you'll have more of it (leftovers great tossed through pasta). This is what I used to do, but nowadays I prefer to strain the sauce because I like how glossy and rich it is - this is how restaurants serve it. You could also skip straining or blitzing, it just means you get little veg lumps in the sauce. All are tasty options, it mainly comes down to visual.
8. TIP: If you strain the sauce, keep the veggies etc in the strainer to make a terrific sauce, they are loaded with flavour even though all juice is squeezed out of them. What I do is make a basic tomato sauce with garlic, onion, canned tomato and water. Then I blitz that with the veggies. Use it to make a killer pasta or lasagna!!
9. Sour sauce? Sounds like there might've been issues with your canned tomatoes (poor quality = overly sour, good quality = sweet). Add a touch of honey or sugar, simmer for few minutes. Also, you didn't rush the carrots/celery sautéing step did you?? Cooking them for 5 minutes sweetens them! :)
10. OTHER COOK OPTIONS:
11. Slow cooker - Follow recipe to step Bring sauce to simmer, scrape bottom of pot to get all brown bits into the liquid. Place shanks in slow cooker, add the sauce. Cook on low for 8 hours. Remove shanks, strain and reduce sauce to desired thickness on stove (if you blitz per Note 5, you won't need to reduce).
12. Pressure Cooker - Follow Slow Cooker steps, cook for 40 minutes on high. Release pressure according to manufacturer directions. Stove - to cook this on the stove, cook for about 2 hours on low, ensuring that you check it at 1 hour then every 30 minutes thereafter to ensure there is enough braising liquid (because liquid evaporates faster on the stove) and the bottom of the pot isn't catching. Turn the lamb shanks twice. You won't get the brown crust, but the flavour is the same!

Slow Cooker Brisket

👥 Servings: 6

Ingredients:

- 1 1 oz. envelope onion soup mix
- 1 tbsp. light brown sugar
- 1 1/2 tsp. kosher salt
- 1/2 tsp. ground black pepper
- 1 3 lb piece of beef brisket (flat cut)
- 8 fresh thyme sprigs
- 8 whole garlic cloves
- 2 bay leaves

- 1 lb. carrots, peeled and cut into 2-inch pieces
- 1 lb. golden baby potatoes
- 3 celery stalks, cut into 1" pieces
- 1 large sweet onion, cut into 8 wedges
- 2 1/2 c. beef stock
- 2 tbsp. Worcestershire sauce
- 2 tbsp. cornstarch

Directions:

1. In a small bowl, combine the soup mix, sugar, salt, and pepper. Sprinkle the mixture over both sides of the brisket and rub it into the meat.

2. Place the meat, fat cap side down, into a 6 to 8-quart slow cooker. Place the thyme sprigs, garlic, and bay leaves on top of brisket. Add the carrots, potatoes, celery, and onion over top.

3. In a liquid measuring cup, whisk together the stock, Worchestershire sauce and cornstarch until the cornstarch is fully dissolved. Pour the liquid into the slow cooker. Cover and cook on high for 5-6 hours, or low for 8 hours until the brisket is tender to slice, but not falling apart.

4. Remove the brisket from the slow cooker and transfer to a cutting board, fat cap side up. Remove and discard the thyme sprigs and bay leaves. Thinly slice the brisket against the grain. Serve alongside the vegetables, drizzled all over with the gravy from the slow cooker.

Slow-cooker Beef Daube

Servings: 4   **Cooking Time:** 7 Hours 10 Mins.

Ingredients:

- 2 tsp olive oil
- 600g Coles Beef Chuck Casserole Steak, trimmed, cut into 3cm pieces
- 1 brown onion, chopped
- 1 carrot, chopped
- 1 celery stalk, chopped
- 2 garlic cloves, finely chopped
- 1 1/2 cups red wine
- 3 tomatoes, chopped
- 3 fresh thyme sprigs
- 7cm strip orange rind
- 2 dried bay leaves
- Mashed potato, to serve
- Steamed green beans, to serve
- Salt, to season

Directions:

1. Heat 1 tbs oil in a large frying pan over medium-high heat. Add beef. Cook, turning occasionally, for 5 minutes or until browned. Transfer to the bowl of a 5.5-litre slow cooker.

2. Heat remaining tbs oil in pan over medium heat. Add onion, carrot, celery and garlic. Cook, stirring occasionally, for 5 minutes or until softened. Transfer to the slow cooker.

3. Add wine, tomato, thyme, orange rind and bay leaves to slow cooker. Stir to combine. Cover with lid. Cook on low for 6 to 8 hours (or on high for 4 hours), removing the lid halfway through cooking.

4. Remove and discard thyme, orange rind and bay leaves. Season with salt and pepper. Serve with mashed potato and green beans.

Notes:

1. Beef daube is traditionally cooked in a terracotta pot called a daubiere, from which it gets its name.

Slow Cooker Beef Topside With Red Wine Gravy

🍴 Servings: 6   🕐 Cooking Time: 6 Hours

Ingredients:

- 1 tbsp black peppercorns
- 1 tbsp English mustard powder
- 2 tbsp chopped rosemary
- 1 tsp celery seeds
- 15g dried porcini mushrooms
- 4 tbsp olive or rapeseed oil
- 1.6kg beef topside, cut into 12 slices
- 600ml hot beef stock
- 1 large carrot, peeled and roughly chopped
- 1 large onion, roughly chopped
- 2 sticks celery, roughly chopped
- 2 tbsp tomato purée
- 200ml red wine
- 1 tbsp cornflour (optional)

Directions:

1. Crush the peppercorns with the mustard, rosemary, celery seeds and a little salt using a pestle and mortar. Blitz the mushrooms to a fine powder in a food processor, then stir them in with 2 tbsp oil and rub all over the beef. Cover and chill for at least 1 hr, but overnight is best.

2. Heat the slow cooker to high and pour in the stock. Heat 2 tbsp oil in a large pan and brown the beef, then put in the slow cooker skin-side up. Fry the carrot, onion and celery in the same pan over a medium-high heat for about 10 mins. Stir in the tomato purée and wine, scraping the bits off the bottom of the pan, then add this to the slow cooker.

3. Cook on low for 6 hrs, then strain the liquid into a pan. Keep the meat and veg covered with foil so they stay warm. Bring the liquid to the boil, then simmer until reduced by a third and season. For thicker gravy, mix the cornflour with 2 tbsp water and whisk into the boiling liquid. Serve the beef with the gravy, along with some mash and greens.

Notes:

1. HAVEN'T GOT A SLOW COOKER?
2. Haven't got a slow cooker? Follow the same method using an ovenproof pan and ensure the stock is boiling when you add it, then put in the oven with a lid on for 2-2½ hrs at 160C/140C fan/gas 3.

Slow Cooker Beef Massaman Curry

Servings: 8   **Cooking Time: 4 Hours 30 Mins.**

Ingredients:

- 3 pounds boneless beef chuck roast
- 3 ½ tablespoons cornstarch, divided
- ½ teaspoon kosher salt
- ½ teaspoon ground black pepper
- 2 tablespoons canola oil
- 6 tablespoons Massaman curry paste
- 1 cup low-sodium beef broth
- 1 (13.5 ounce) can unsweetened coconut cream
- 1 pound baby Yukon Gold potatoes
- 2 tablespoons cold water
- 1 lime, zested and juiced
- 3 cups cooked jasmine rice
- ½ cup roasted cashews
- 1 cup chopped fresh cilantro leaves and stems
- 1 medium Fresno chile, thinly sliced
- additional lime wedges, for serving, if desired

Directions:

1. Pat beef dry with paper towels, trim, and cut into 1 1/2- to 2-inch pieces. Place in a bowl with 2 tablespoons cornstarch, salt, and pepper; toss to coat beef evenly.

2. Heat oil in a large nonstick skillet over medium-high heat. Add half of the beef and cook, turning often, until beef is browned on all sides, about 6 minutes (do not overcrowd the skillet to ensure browning). Repeat process with remaining beef, using any residual oil in the skillet. (Do not wipe skillet clean.) Place browned beef in an ungreased 6-quart slow cooker.

3. Once all beef has been browned, lower heat to medium and add curry paste, stirring to release any browned bits from the skillet. Add beef broth and coconut cream to skillet, stirring to combine ingredients. Pour mixture over beef in slow cooker. Add potatoes to slow cooker; cover and cook on HIGH for 4 hours, or LOW for 6 hours, or until beef is very tender when pierced with a fork.

4. Remove beef and potatoes to a large bowl, and carefully pour liquid from slow cooker into a heatproof glass measuring cup or bowl and allow to stand until fat settles on top of liquid, about 2 minutes. Remove fat from the surface of the liquid with a ladle and discard.

5. Pour remaining liquid into a saucepan and bring to a boil, undisturbed, over medium-high heat. Whisk remaining 1 1/2 tablespoons cornstarch with 2 tablespoons cold water together in a small bowl; add to boiling liquid in saucepan, whisking until mixture thickens, 2 to 5 minutes. Return meat and potatoes to thickened sauce; stir in lime zest and juice.

6. Serve family-style, or place 1/2 cup rice into each of 6 bowls, spoon 1 1/3 cups beef, potatoes, and sauce mixture over rice, and garnish each portion with cashews, cilantro, sliced chile, and a lime wedge.

Slow-cooker Lamb's Liver, Bacon And Onions Recipe

 Servings: 8   Cooking Time: 8 Hours

Ingredients:

- 2 tbsp unsalted butter
- 4 rashers smoked back bacon, cut into strips
- 450g pack sliced lamb's liver
- 3 tbsp plain flour
- 1 onion, thinly sliced
- 1 beef stock cube, made up to 500ml
- 1 tsp Worcestershire sauce
- 1 bay leaf
- mashed potato and peas, to serve (optional)

Directions:

1. Heat a nonstick frying pan with half the butter over a medium heat and fry the bacon for 3-4 mins until crispy. Remove with a slotted spoon and set aside on kitchen paper.

2. Pat dry the livers, then toss with 2 tbsp flour and plenty of seasoning. Shake of any excess, then cook in the bacon fat over a medium heat for 1-2 mins each side until browned. Set aside.

3. Add the remaining butter to the pan with the onion and cook for 8-10 mins over a medium-low heat until lightly golden. Stir in the bacon and liver.

4. Mix the remaining flour with 2 tbsp stock. Transfer the liver mix to a slow-cooker. Set to low, then pour in the remaining stock, the Worcestershire sauce, bay leaf and the flour paste. Stir well, then cook for 6-8 hrs until the liver is tender and the sauce silky. Serve with mash and peas, if you like.

5. *Liver is high in vitamin A and should not be consumed by women planning pregnancy or during pregnancy.

6. Freezing

7. In order to enjoy optimum flavour and quality, frozen items are best used within 3 months of their freezing date.

Tender Salsa Beef

 Servings: 8   Cooking Time: 8 Hours

Ingredients:

- 1-1/2 pounds beef stew meat, cut into 3/4-inch cubes
- 2 cups salsa
- 1 tablespoon brown sugar
- 1 tablespoon reduced-sodium soy sauce
- 1 garlic clove, minced
- 4 cups hot cooked brown rice
- Sliced jalapeno peppers, optional

Directions:

1. In a 3-qt. slow cooker, combine the beef, salsa, brown sugar, soy sauce and garlic. Cover and cook on low 8-10 hours, until meat is tender. Using a slotted spoon, serve beef with rice and, if desired, sliced jalapeno peppers.

Slow-cooker Sticky Chinese Pork

Servings: 6   **Cooking Time: 4 Hours 40 Mins.**

Ingredients:

- 1.8kg boneless pork shoulder
- 1 tsp five-spice powder
- 1/4 cup peanut oil
- 5 spring onions, trimmed, halved, plus extra sliced to serve
- 10cm piece fresh ginger, sliced
- 1 cinnamon stick
- 4 garlic cloves, bruised
- 1 cup shao hsing (chinese rice wine)
- 1/3 cup light soy sauce
- 1 cup chicken stock
- 2 tbsp brown sugar
- 2 tbsp honey
- 2 bunches pak choy, halved lengthways
- 4 long red chillies, halved lengthways
- Sesame seeds, to serve
- Fresh coriander leaves, to serve
- Steamed jasmine rice, to serve
- Lemon wedges, to serve

Directions:

1. Remove string from pork. Remove and discard rind from pork. Rub pork all over with five-spice powder. Heat 1 tablespoon oil in a large frying pan over medium-high heat. Add pork. Cook for 4 minutes each side or until browned.

2. Combine onion, ginger, cinnamon, garlic, shao hsing, 1/4 cup soy sauce, stock and sugar in the base of a 5.5-litre slow cooker. Place pork in slow cooker. Cover. Cook on HIGH for 4 hours 30 minutes or until pork is tender

3. Preheat oven to 220C/200C fan-forced. Line a baking tray with baking paper. Transfer pork to prepared tray. Combine honey and remaining soy in a small bowl. Brush pork with half the honey mixture. Bake for 6 to 8 minutes or until sticky, brushing with remaining honey mixture halfway through. Cool for 15 minutes.

4. Meanwhile, add pak choy to slow cooker. Cook for 5 minutes or until pak choy is just tender.

5. Heat remaining oil in a small frying pan over medium-high heat. Add chillies. Cook, turning occasionally, for 4 minutes or until charred. Remove from heat.

Slow-cooker Cuban Pulled Beef

👥 Servings: 8   🕐 Cooking Time: 8 Hours

Ingredients:

- 1 tbsp extra virgin olive oil
- 1.5kg gravy beef
- 1 brown onion, finely chopped
- 2 red capsicums, finely chopped
- 2 garlic cloves, crushed
- 2 tsp dried oregano
- 2 dried bay leaves
- 2 tsp caster sugar
- 1 tsp dried chilli flakes
- 1 tsp ground allspice
- 700g jar gluten-free tomato passata
- 1/3 cup red wine vinegar

- 2 cups white long-grain rice
- 400g can black beans, drained, rinsed
- 2 tbsp chopped fresh coriander
- 1 green onion, finely chopped
- 2 tbsp lime juice, plus wedges to serve
- Chimichurri
- 1 1/2 cups fresh flat-leaf parsley leaves
- 1/2 cup fresh coriander leaves
- 1/2 cup fresh oregano leaves
- 2 garlic cloves, halved
- 1/4 cup extra virgin olive oil
- 2 tbsp red wine vinegar

Directions:

1. Heat oil in a frying pan over medium-high heat. Cook beef, in batches, for 5 minutes or until browned. Transfer to slow cooker. Top with brown onion, capsicum, garlic, oregano, bay leaves, sugar, chilli, allspice, passata and vinegar. Season. Cover. Cook on low for 8 hours, turning beef in sauce halfway through cooking.
2. Make Chimichurri: Process herbs and garlic in a small food processor until finely chopped. Add oil and vinegar. Process until combined. Set aside.
3. Cook rice following packet directions, adding beans in the last 2 minutes of cooking. Drain. Transfer to a bowl. Stir in coriander and green onion. Season. Using 2 forks, shred beef. Stir in lime juice. Serve beef with rice, chimichurri and lime wedges.

Slow Cooker Red Beans And Rice

👥 Servings: 8-10

Ingredients:

- 1 pound dried red beans
- 1/2 pound andouille sausage, chopped
- 3 ribs celery, chopped
- 1 smoked ham shank
- 1 medium onion, chopped
- 1 large green bell pepper, chopped
- 1 tablespoon chili powder
- 1 teaspoon ground cumin
- 1 teaspoon garlic powder

- 1/2 teaspoon cayenne
- 1/2 teaspoon onion powder
- 1/2 teaspoon paprika
- 1/2 teaspoon brown sugar
- Kosher salt
- 4 cups chicken stock
- 8 cups cooked long-grain white rice, for serving
- 4 scallions, chopped

Directions:

1. In a slow cooker, combine the beans, andouille, celery, ham shank, onions, bell peppers, chili powder, cumin, garlic powder, cayenne, onion powder, paprika, brown sugar and 2 teaspoons salt. Add the chicken stock and 2 cups water and stir to mix.
2. Cook on the high setting until the beans are tender, 6 to 8 hours. Season with salt. Serve with rice, topped with scallions.

Slow Cooker Lamb Stew

👥 Servings: 6   🕐 Cooking Time: 5 Hours 30 Mins.

Ingredients:

- 1 (2lb 5oz) diced lamb leg
- 2 onions, finely sliced
- 500 ml (17 fl oz) chicken stock
- 400 g (14oz) tin chickpeas, drained and rinsed
- 1 small cauliflower
- 50 g (2oz) dried cherries
- 2 tbsp. cornflour
- FOR THE MARINADE
- 1 tsp. olive oil
- 50 g (2oz) harissa
- 3 garlic cloves, crushed
- 2 tsp. each ground cumin, smoked paprika and

- flaked sea salt
- 1 tsp. each ground coriander, fennel seeds, ground cinnamon and freshly ground black pepper
- 2 tbsp. each honey and pomegranate molasses
- Finely grated zest of 1 lemon
- TO SERVE
- 200 g (7oz) Greek yoghurt
- 25 g (1oz) fresh mint leaves, finely chopped
- 1 garlic clove
- 100 g (3 ½oz) pomegranate seeds

Directions:

1. In a large bowl stir together the marinade ingredients. Add the lamb, stir to coat, cover and chill overnight.

2. The next day add the lamb and any juices to the pan of a slow cooker. Stir in the onions and slowly add the hot chicken stock, stirring the entire time. Cover with a lid and cook on high for 4hr.

3. Cut the cauliflower into large florets and chop the stalk and set aside the leaves. Add the chickpeas, cauliflower florets and chopped stalk. Cover and cook for a further 1hr.

4. In a small bowl, stir together the cornflour with 1tbsp water to form a thin paste. Add to stew, stirring constantly as you tip the mixture in, then add the cauliflower leaves and dried cherries and fold to combine. Cover and cook for another 30min.

5. Stir the yoghurt together with most of the mint, garlic and some seasoning. Serve stew with the minty yoghurt drizzled over, the extra mint and pomegranate seeds scattered on top and couscous on the side.

Slow Cooker Bolognese Sauce

Servings: 6   **Cooking Time: 7 Hours**

Ingredients:

- 2 lbs ground beef
- 1 white onion Diced
- 4 cloves garlic Minced
- ½ cup red wine
- 56 oz crushed tomatoes (two 28-oz. cans)
- 1 cup beef stock or beef broth
- 4 Tbsp. tomato paste

- 2 Tbsp. Italian seasoning
- 1 tsp. salt
- 1 tsp. black pepper
- 1 Tbsp. brown sugar
- For serving
- 16 oz dried spaghetti uncooked

Directions:

1. In a large skillet over medium high heat, brown the ground beef until cooked completely. Add the cooked ground beef to the bottom of the slow cooker pot.

2. In the same skillet over medium heat, add the onion and garlic and cook until the onion is translucent, pour in the red wine and bring to a simmer. Let simmer for 2-3 minutes to burn off the alcohol. Pour the red wine and onions into the slow cooker with the ground beef.

3. To the slow cooker, add the rest of the ingredients (not including the spaghetti) and stir. Cook on HIGH for 3-4 hours or LOW for 6-7 hours. During the last 20 minutes of cook time, cook the spaghetti according to package instructions on the stove top.

4. Serve the bolognese with the spaghetti by mixing some of the sauce into the spaghetti and then pouring more over the top.

5. Top with parmesan cheese and fresh basil if desired, enjoy!

Notes:

1. Store the sauce in the refrigerator for up to 3 days in an airtight container, or store in the freezer in a freezer safe container for up to 4 months.

2. Let defrost overnight in the refrigerator and reheat on the stove top.

3. For red wine to cook with use, cabernet sauvignon, pinot noir, or merlot.

4. White sugar can be used in place of the brown sugar, I like to use the brown sugar because it adds a deeper richer flavor to the sauce instead of just using white sugar as sweetener.

Slow-roast Pork Belly With Celeriac & Pear Mash

Servings: 4   **Cooking Time: 2 Hours 30 Mins.**

Ingredients:

- 1 ½kg pork belly, skin scored
- 3 rosemary sprigs, leaves stripped
- 2 tsp coarse sea salt crystals
- 10 black peppercorns
- purple sprouting broccoli, steamed, to serve
- For the mash

- 750g celeriac, cubed
- 1 large potato, cubed
- 2 ripe pears, peeled and cubed
- 3 tbsp double cream
- large knob of butter

Directions:

1. Heat oven to 220C/200C fan/gas 7. Take the pork out of the fridge and pat the skin dry. Put the rosemary leaves, salt and pepper in a mini chopper and grind together (or do this with a mortar and pestle). Rub the rosemary salt all over the pork, making sure it gets into the cuts in the skin. Sit the pork in a large roasting tin, ideally on a rack, and roast for 30 mins.

2. Reduce heat to 170C/150 fan/gas 3 and roast for 1½ hrs more. Turn oven back up to 220C/200C fan/gas 7 and roast for 20-30 mins to crisp. Leave to rest on a board for 10 mins before carving.

3. When the pork is nearly ready to come out, put the celeriac and potato in a large pan of water, bring to the boil and cook for 10 mins until just tender. Add the pears and cook for 2 mins more. Drain well, then mash until smooth – a mouli or potato ricer does this job best. Beat in a splash of cream and some butter, and serve with the pork and broccoli.

Easy Lamb Chop Casserole

Servings: 4   **Cooking Time: 8 Hours 10 Mins.**

Ingredients:

- 1kg lamb chop, fat trimmed
- 45g French onion soup mix
- 425g canned crushed tomatoes

- 3 tbs mixed herbs
- 1 1/2 tsp garlic crushed optional

Directions:

1. Place all the ingredients in a slow cooker and cook on low for 8 hours or on high for 3-4 hours.

2. Serve with mashed potatoes and steamed vegetables.

Notes:

1. I use forequarter lamb chops.

Slow Cooker Honey & Mustard Pork Loin

Servings: 4-6   **Cooking Time: 5 Hours-6 Hours**

Ingredients:

- 1½ tsp fennel seeds
- 2 garlic cloves
- 5-6 thyme sprigs
- 2 tbsp rapeseed or olive oil
- 1.8kg pork loin, skin removed and fat well scored (cut from the thicker end of the joint)
- 300g shallots
- 1 small celeriac, peeled, quartered and cut into
- chunks
- 2 eating apples (such as Braeburn or Cox), peeled, cored and cut into wedges
- 150ml white wine
- 250ml chicken or pork stock
- 1 tbsp honey
- 1 tbsp Dijon mustard

Directions:

1. Lightly crush the fennel, garlic and the leaves of 3 thyme sprigs together in a pestle and mortar. Add 1 tbsp oil and season well, then bash to a rough paste. Rub the mixture all over the pork, then cover and chill for at least 2 hrs or up to 24 hrs.

2. Set the slow cooker to low. Tip the shallots into a heatproof bowl and pour a kettleful of boiling water. Leave to soak for 2 mins, then drain and rinse under cold water until cool enough to handle (this will make them easier to peel). Cut off the roots and remove the papery skins.

3. Heat the remaining oil in a frying pan or flameproof casserole that's large enough to fit the pork joint. Brown the shallots for a few minutes over a medium heat, then tip into the slow cooker. Add the celeriac and apples, then season well and mix.

4. Put the pork in the pan and brown really well on all sides, then transfer to the slow cooker fat-side up on top of the vegetable mixture. Pour the wine into the pan and bubble for 1 min. Add the stock, honey and mustard and bubble for 1 min more, then pour the mixture over the pork. Cover and cook on low for 5-6 hrs, turning the meat and stirring the veg halfway through cooking, if you can.

5. Lift the pork out of the slow cooker, wrap and leave to rest for 10 mins before carving. Serve with the cooked vegetables and some greens, if you like.

6. Recipe tip

7. On a high setting, the pork should take 3-4 hrs to cook. Smaller slow cookers will take less time than larger ones.

Slow Roast Honey & Sesame Duck

Servings: Cooking Time: 2 Hours 30 Mins.

Ingredients:

- For the duck
- 1.5-2kg/3lb 5oz-4lb 8oz oven-ready duck
- 2 tsp coarse sea salt (see 'Try' below)
- 4 tbsp clear honey
- 2 tsp sesame seed

- For the red wine sauce
- 125ml red wine
- 150ml chicken stock (or water with a small sprinkling of chicken stock cube)
- knob of butter

Directions:

1. Heat oven to 160C/fan 140C/gas 3. Score the duck breast skin with a sharp knife. This helps release excess fat from the skin as the bird roasts. Season the duck with the sea salt and pepper, then sit it on a rack set in a roasting tray and roast for 1½ hrs. Remove the bird from the oven and pour off the excess fat collected in the tray.

2. Return the duck to the roasting tray, then spoon 3 tbsp of the honey over to cover the breasts and legs. Roast the duck for a further hr, basting with the honey every 10-15 mins. Sprinkle the sesame seeds on top during the final 10 mins of roasting.

3. Once cooked, remove duck from the roasting tray, and allow it to rest for 10-15 mins. Spoon the remaining tbsp of honey over the duck as it rests.

4. Meanwhile, make the sauce. Pour off any excess fat from the roasting tin, leaving behind a couple of tbsp of the honey and duck juices. Heat the roasting tray on top of the stove. Once the contents sizzle and become well caramelised, pour in the red wine, then boil for a few mins to reduce by about a third. Pour in the chicken stock (or water and stock cube), then simmer for several mins, also allowing it to slightly reduce to strengthen the flavour. Finish off the sauce (which is quite loose) with the knob of butter (for thicker gravy see 'Try' below). Season with salt and pepper and strain through a fine sieve, if you like.

5. Now finsih it in style: Gary say's: I prefer to serve just the half duck on the plate. To do this, remove the duck breasts and legs from the breast bone by cutting either side of the breast bone, following its natural line. Drizzle any excess honey juices over and offer all accompaniments separately.

Notes:

1. CRISPY SKIN
2. Salting the duck really well before roasting draws the moisture out, which helps to crisp up the skin.
3. THICKER GRAVY
4. If you prefer a thicker gravy, instead of adding a knob of butter when finishing it, mix 1 tsp cornflour with a few drops of water or red wine and stir into the gravy, simmering until thickened.

Slow Cooker Hungarian Goulash

👥 Servings: 6

Ingredients:

- 2 lbs. cubed stew meat or a chuck roast cubed
- ¼ cup all purpose flour
- 2 tsp. salt divided
- ½ tsp. black pepper
- 28 oz. can crushed tomatoes
- 2 medium potatoes cut into 1/2 inch chunks
- 2 carrots diced
- 1 red pepper seeded and cut into 1/2 inch pieces
- 1 green pepper seeded and cut into 1/2 inch pieces
- 2 large onions chopped
- 3½ Tbsp. sweet Hungarian paprika
- 1 tsp. marjoram
- 1½ Tbsp. minced garlic about 4 plump cloves
- ¾ tsp. crushed caraway seeds
- 4 cups low sodium beef broth
- 6 oz. can tomato paste
- 2 bay leaves
- Optional Ingredients:
- fresh parsley 1/4 cup plus more as garnish
- sour cream 1/2 cup or to taste.
- Buttered egg noodles

Directions:

1. Place the roast pieces in a bowl and toss with the flour, salt and pepper until coated. Add the beef to the slow cooker, then add the crushed tomatoes, potatoes, carrots, red and green pepper, onion, paprika, garlic, marjoram, and caraway seed. (Also the fresh parsley if using.)
2. Pour the beef broth over stew and add the bay leaves.
3. Set on high for 6 hours or low for 9 hours. Add additional broth if needed.
4. Last half hour or so remove some liquid to a medium bowl and whisk in the tomato paste. Return that to the Slow Cooker and cook for the last half hour to thicken. Add additional remaining salt if needed.
5. **If adding sour cream, remove some of the stew broth during the last 5 minutes and slow stir in the sour cream to temper, avoiding curdling and then stir into the slow cooker.
6. Serve the goulash over egg noodles and garnish with fresh parsley.

Notes:

1. This dish is extra delicious with beer or you can use red wine. If you prefer not to use alcohol you can just use beef broth which is also very delicious. Use one cup of beer or red wine (take away one cup of broth from recipe.)
2. This recipe calls for a lot of paprika and yes, that is correct. The paprika and caraway is what gives this dish its unique flavor.

Slow-cooker Beef Cheeks In Red Wine

👥 Servings: 6   🕐 Cooking Time: 8 Hours 20 Mins.

Ingredients:

- 1/4 cup plain flour
- 1.2kg beef cheeks
- 2 tbsp olive oil
- 2 medium brown onions, cut into wedges
- 6 cloves garlic, halved
- 2 medium carrots, coarsely chopped
- 1 cup (250ml) Shiraz red wine
- 2 cups (500ml) Massel beef stock
- 2 tbsp brown sugar
- 2 tbsp tomato paste
- 2 bay leaves
- 3 sprigs fresh thyme
- 40g Coles Australian Salted Butter
- 6 shiitake mushrooms, halved
- 6 medium swiss brown mushrooms, halved
- 12 small button mushrooms
- Salt, to season

Directions:

1. Season flour with salt and pepper. Place flour in a large snap-lock bag. Add half the beef. Seal. Shake to coat. Remove from bag, shaking off excess flour. Transfer to plate. Repeat with remaining beef.
2. Heat oil in a large frying pan over medium-high heat. Cook beef in batches, for 3 minutes each side or until browned. Transfer to a plate.
3. Add onion, garlic and carrots to pan. Cook, stirring, for 3 minutes or until golden. Place half the onion mixture in the bowl of a 5 litre slow-cooker. Top with beef and remaining onion mixture.
4. Add wine, stock, sugar, paste and herbs to frying pan. Bring to the boil then pour over beef in slow-cooker.
5. Add butter to pan, then mushrooms. Cook, stirring, for 3 minutes or until browned. Add to beef.
6. Cover with lid. Turn slow-cooker on low. Cook for 8 hours or until beef is tender. (Alternately, turn slow-cooker on high and cook for 4 hours). Sprinkle with fresh thyme and serve with garlic mash, steamed asparagus and green beans.

Slow Roasted Tuscan Pork Recipe

 Servings: 6-8   🕐 Cooking Time: 5 Hours

Ingredients:

- 2.5kg (5lb) pork leg joint
- 3 tbsp olive oil
- 4 cloves garlic cut into slivers
- 2 tbsp fennel seeds
- 2 tsp dried chilli flakes
- 2 tbsp dried oregano
- 2 tbsp fresh rosemary, finely chopped

- For the mint caper sauce
- 2 tbsp tiny capers
- 2 shallots
- 20g (3/4oz) fresh mint, stems removed
- 1 garlic clove
- 3 tbsp balsamic vinegar
- 4 tbsp Tesco Finest extra virgin olive oil

Directions:

1. Preheat the oven 140°C. Take a sharp knife and cut small slits into the meat. Insert the slivers of garlic all over the meat. Mix together the herbs and chilli. Rub the pork roast with 1 tbsp of olive oil and salt and pepper.
2. In a very large frying pan, sear the meat on all sides until browned. Rub the remaining oil over the pork and then roll in the herbs. Arrange on a roasting rack over a roasting tin. Place in the hot oven and cook for approx 4-5 hours.
3. The meat will be tender and fall apart when the string is removed. Slice the pork and place on a platter with rosemary sprigs and other fresh herbs. Serve with sauce and some crispy or mashed potatoes.
4. To make the sauce
5. Finely chop the capers, shallots, garlic, and mint and place in a small bowl. Add the vinegar, oil, salt and pepper and a large pinch of sugar. Mix well and pour into a serving jug.

Slow-roasted Lamb Shoulder With Salsa Verde Marinade

 Servings: 4

Ingredients:

- 1/2 bunch each flat-leaf parsley and mint leaves picked
- 1 bunch tarragon, leaves picked
- 2 anchovy llets in oil, drained
- 1 tbs capers in brine, rinsed, drained

- Juice of 1 lemon
- 1 garlic clove, crushed
- 140ml mild extra virgin olive oil
- 1.8kg boneless butterfied lamb shoulder

Directions:

1. Whiz all ingredients, except lamb, in a food processor until smooth. Season. Place lamb on a baking tray and coat with half the salsa verde (cover and chill remaining salsa verde until ready to serve). Cover lamb and chill overnight.
2. The next day, preheat oven to 200°C. Bring lamb to room temperature, then place in a roasting pan and season with salt.
3. Roast for 1 hour, then reduce oven to 150°C. Place a small ovenproof bowl of water in the base of the oven to create steam (this will help prevent the lamb from burning).
4. Roast for 31/2 hours or until lamb is very tender. Remove from oven and rest, loosely covered with foil, for 20 minutes.
5. Carve lamb and drizzle over remaining salsa verde to serve.

OTHER FAVORITE RECIPES

Pizza Quinoa Casserole

🍴 Servings: 6   🕐 Cooking Time: 10 Mins.

Ingredients:

- 1 tablespoon olive oil
- 1/2 pound Italian turkey sausage links, casings removed
- 1 small red onion, sliced
- 2 cups sliced fresh mushrooms
- 2 cups chicken broth
- 1 cup quinoa, rinsed
- 2 cups pizza sauce

- 1 package (6 ounces) sliced turkey pepperoni
- 1 medium green pepper, chopped
- 1/2 cup shredded part-skim mozzarella cheese
- 1/2 cup shredded Parmesan cheese
- Optional: Minced fresh basil, sliced olives, oil-packed sun-dried tomatoes (drained), banana peppers and red pepper flakes

Directions:

1. Select saute setting on a 6-qt. electric pressure cooker. Adjust for medium heat; add oil. When oil is hot, add sausage and onion; cook and stir until sausage is no longer pink and onion is tender, 5-7 minutes, breaking up sausage into crumbles; drain. Press cancel.

2. Stir in mushrooms and broth. Add quinoa (do not stir). Lock lid; close pressure-release valve. Adjust to pressure-cook on high for 2 minutes. Quick-release pressure.

3. Stir in pizza sauce, pepperoni and green pepper; cover and let stand until pepper softens slightly, 5-10 minutes. Sprinkle servings with cheeses. If desired, serve with optional toppings.

4. Slow-cooker option: In a large skillet, heat oil over medium heat; cook sausage and onion until sausage is no longer pink, 5-7 minutes, breaking up sausage into large crumbles. Drain.

5. Transfer sausage and onion to a 4- or 5-qt. slow cooker. Stir in mushrooms, broth and quinoa. Cook, covered, on low for 5 hours; stir in pizza sauce, pepperoni and green pepper. Cook, covered, on low until pepper is tender, about 1 hour longer. Sprinkle servings with cheeses. If desired, serve with optional toppings.

Pasta E Fagioli

 Servings: 6-8   Cooking Time: 7 Hours-9 Hours

Ingredients:

- 200g dried borlotti or cannellini beans, soaked for 6-8 hours
- 2 onions, cut into 1cm chunks
- 2 medium carrots, cut into 1cm chunks
- 3 celery stalks, cut into 1cm chunks
- 2 tbsp extra virgin olive oil, plus extra to serve (optional)
- 4 garlic cloves, crushed
- 1 litre fresh vegetable stock

- 400g can plum tomatoes
- 2 tbsp brown rice miso
- 6 rosemary sprigs
- 4 bay leaves
- 150g ditaloni rigati or other small pasta shapes
- 200g cavolo nero, stalks finely chopped and leaves torn
- 30g vegan parmesan, grated, to serve (optional)

Directions:

1. Drain the beans and bring to the boil in a pan of salted water. Cook for 10 mins, drain, rinse and put in a slow cooker with the onions, carrots and celery.

2. Stir in the olive oil, garlic, stock, tomatoes, half a can of water and the miso. Tie the herbs together with kitchen string and add these as well. Season. Cover and cook on low for 6-8 hrs, until the beans are cooked through and all of the veg is really tender.

3. Remove and discard the herbs and stir in the pasta. Cover and cook on high for another 30 mins. Add the cavolo nero stalks and leaves and cook for a final 30-40 mins, or until the pasta is cooked through and the greens are tender. Serve scattered with the cheese and drizzled with a little more olive oil, if you like.

Notes:

1. USE CANS IF PREFERRED
2. You could use 2 x 400g cans drained and rinsed beans in place of dried. Just skip the cooking in step 1.

Slow Cooker Mac 'n' Cheese

 Servings: 4   Cooking Time: 1 Hours 15 Mins.

Ingredients:

- 200g macaroni
- 200g cheddar, finely grated
- 1/4 cup plain flour
- 3 cups Massel chicken style liquid stock

- 25g butter, chopped
- 2/3 cup frozen peas (optional)
- Baby rocket, to serve

Directions:

1. Place macaroni, cheddar and flour in a 3L (12 cup) slow-cooker. Using hands, mix until well combined.

2. Bring stock to the boil in a small saucepan over high heat. Pour over pasta. Add butter and stir to mix well. Cover and cook on high for 1 1/4 hours, stirring after 45 minutes to break up any clumps of pasta.

3. Stir in peas. Stand for 1-2 minutes. Season with pepper. Serve with rocket

Slow Cooker Butter Halloumi Curry

👪 Servings: 4   🕐 Cooking Time: 5 Mins.

Ingredients:

- FOR THE SAUCE
- 8 cardamom pods
- 1 tsp. fenugreek seeds
- 2 tsp. cumin seeds
- 1/2 tsp. cayenne pepper
- 1 tsp. ground turmeric
- 2 garlic cloves, chopped
- 2 1/2 cm piece fresh root ginger, peeled and grated
- 40 g butter or ghee, melted
- 1 onion, chopped
- 400 g tin chopped tomatoes
- 1 tbsp. tomato puree
- 1 tbsp. mango chutney, plus extra (optional) to serve
- FOR THE CURRY
- 500 g halloumi, cut into 2cm cubes
- 1 cinnamon stick
- 100 ml double cream
- Large handful fresh coriander leaves, roughly chopped

Directions:

1. With a pestle and mortar, bash open cardamom pods and crush briefly until seeds come out. Pick out and discard the pod husks. Add the fenugreek, cumin, cayenne and turmeric to mortar, then crush spices with the pestle until ground to a medium coarseness.
2. Put the ground spices in a blender, along with the remaining sauce ingredients and blend until smooth. Transfer sauce to the slow cooker and stir in the halloumi and cinnamon stick.
3. Cover with the lid and cook on low for 3-5hr (timings may vary between slow cooker models). Remove and discard the cinnamon, stir through the cream, recover the lid and heat briefly. Check seasoning and sprinkle with coriander. Serve with rice and mango chutney, if you like.

Slow-cooked Summer Blush

👪 Servings: 20   🕐 Cooking Time: 2 Hours

Ingredients:

- 15 red peppers, quartered and deseeded
- 15 ripe plum tomatoes, quartered
- 2 heads of garlic, broken down into individual unpeeled cloves
- 6 tbsp extra-virgin olive oil
- 1 tbsp golden caster sugar
- 3 tbsp red wine vinegar
- handful thyme sprigs
- 3 handfuls basil leaves, roughly torn

Directions:

1. Heat oven to 160C/fan 140C/gas 3. In a large, deep roasting pan, gently toss everything, except the basil, together, then season.
2. Place the vegetables in the oven, then roast for 2 hrs, undisturbed. Remove from the oven and leave to cool. If you want, drain the vegetables before serving and serve their juice on the side, or simply stir through the basil and correct the seasoning.
3. The vegetables can be roasted up to 2 days ahead. Cover and leave in the fridge, but bring out at least 4 hours before serving so the vegetables are served at room temperature.

Slow-cooker Sausage And Butter Bean Casserole Recipe

👪 Servings: 6

Ingredients:

- 2 tbsp olive oil
- 454g pack 50% less fat Cumberland sausages
- 2 red onions, cut into wedges
- 2 celery sticks, trimmed and sliced
- 1 garlic clove, sliced
- 150g mushrooms, quartered
- 150g pack Tendersweet carrots
- 1 leek, trimmed and sliced
- ½ tsp crushed chillies
- 2 x 400g tins butter beans, drained and rinsed
- 400g tin chopped tomatoes
- 300ml red wine
- 1 chicken stock cube, made up to 800ml
- 10g fresh rosemary, leaves only
- 4 tbsp cornflour, mixed with 5 tbsp water
- green beans and crusty bread, to serve (optional)

Directions:

1. Heat the oil in a heavy-based frying pan over a medium-high heat and fry the sausages for 6-7 mins, turning frequently, until golden. Transfer to a 2.5ltr or bigger slow-cooker using a slotted spoon.

2. Add the onions, celery, garlic and mushrooms to the pan and cook in the remaining oil for 4-5 mins over a medium-high heat, stirring occasionally, until beginning to soften. Transfer to the slow-cooker with the carrots and leek.

3. Mix the remaining ingredients together in a bowl, then add to the slow-cooker and season well. Cook on high for 3 hrs or until thick and bubbling.

4. Spoon into bowls and serve with green beans and crusty bread to mop up the juices, if you like.

5. Cook's tip: No slow-cooker? Follow the method to brown the sausages and veg, then put in a 2ltr casserole dish, cover and bake at gas 6, 200℃, fan 180℃ for 2 hrs.

Slow Cooker Mac & Cheese

👪 Servings: 8-10

Ingredients:

- 1 lb. elbow macaroni
- 1/2 c. (1 stick) melted butter
- 4 c. shredded cheddar cheese
- 4 oz. cream cheese, cut into cubes
- 1/2 c. freshly grated grated Parmesan
- 2 (12-oz.) cans evaporated milk
- 2 c. whole milk
- 1/2 tsp. garlic powder
- 1/8 tsp. paprika
- kosher salt
- Freshly ground black pepper
- Finely chopped chives, for garnish (optional)

Directions:

1. Combine macaroni, butter, cheddar cheese, cream cheese, Parmesan, evaporated milk, whole milk, garlic powder, and paprika in a slow cooker. Season with salt and pepper.

2. Cook on high until the pasta is cooked through and the sauce has thickened, 2 to 3 hours, checking after 2 hours, then every 20 minutes after.

3. Garnish with chives before serving, if using.

Chili Coney Dogs

 Servings: 8   Cooking Time: 4 Hours

Ingredients:

- 1 pound lean ground beef (90% lean)
- 1 can (15 ounces) tomato sauce
- 1/2 cup water
- 2 tablespoons Worcestershire sauce
- 1 tablespoon dried minced onion
- 1/2 teaspoon garlic powder
- 1/2 teaspoon ground mustard
- 1/2 teaspoon chili powder
- 1/2 teaspoon pepper
- Dash cayenne pepper
- 8 hot dogs
- 8 hot dog buns, split
- Optional toppings: Shredded cheddar cheese, relish and chopped onion

Directions:

1. In a large skillet, cook beef over medium heat until no longer pink, 6-8 minutes, breaking into crumbles; drain. Stir in tomato sauce, water, Worcestershire sauce, dried minced onion and seasonings.
2. Place hot dogs in a 3-qt. slow cooker; top with beef mixture. Cook, covered, on low 4-5 hours or until heated through. Serve on buns with toppings as desired.

Slow Cooker Gammon In Cider

Servings: 6

Ingredients:

- 1.5kg gammon joint
- 1 carrot, quartered
- 1 stick celery, halved
- 1 onion, quartered
- 1 tbsp black peppercorns
- 400ml dry cider
- GLAZE
- 2 tbsp wholegrain mustard
- 1 tbsp runny honey

Directions:

1. Heat the slow cooker to low. Put in the gammon joint and tuck the veg around it. Scatter over the peppercorns and pour over the cider.
2. Put on the lid and cook for 4 hours. Remove the gammon and cool a little. Discard the veg and cooking liquid.
3. Heat the oven to 190C/fan 170C/gas 5. When the skin is cool enough to handle carefully cut it away, leaving a layer of fat. Score the fat and sit the gammon in a foil-lined baking tray. Mix together the mustard and honey, and spread all over the fat. Bake for 30 minutes or until sticky and glazed.

Graham Campbell's Roast Gammon With Sweet Potato Roasties Recipe

Servings: 6   **Cooking Time: 5 Hours 30 Mins.**

Ingredients:

- For the roast gammon
- 1.3kg (2 1/2lb) unsmoked Gammon joint
- 2 carrots, peeled
- 2 onions, peeled
- 4 garlic cloves, bruised
- 3 celery sticks
- 2 bay leaves
- 4 sprigs of thyme
- For the glaze
- 12 cardamom pods
- 4 tsp ground cinnamon
- 2 tsp mild chilli powder
- 2 1/2 tbsp five-spice powder
- ¼ tsp ground cloves
- 100ml soy sauce

- 90g honey
- ¼ tbsp salt
- For the sweet potato roasties
- 600g sweet potato
- 1 sprig fresh rosemary, finely chopped
- 50ml (2fl oz) olive oil
- 1 pinch salt
- 1 pinch pepper
- For the bacon sprouts
- 300g (10oz) brussel sprouts
- 60g (2 1/2oz) bacon, diced
- 1 pinch nutmeg
- 1 dash olive oil
- 1 knob butter
- 1 pinch salt

Directions:

1. Leave the gammon to soak overnight in a large tub of water to reduce the saltiness. The next day, drain the water and leave the meat in the tub under a running tap to rinse for 5 minutes.

2. Add 1 carrot, 1 onion, 2 celery sticks and 3 garlic cloves to a large saucepan. Place the gammon in the pan along with the bay leaf and thyme. Cover with water, and place a lid on the pan. Bring to the boil.

3. When the water is boiling, reduce the heat and simmer for 3 hours. Then take the pan off the heat and leave the gammon to cool.

4. Preheat the oven to Gas Mark 4, 170°C, fan 150°C.

5. Make the spice mix by grinding the cardamom pods in a pestle and mortar until broken up. Place in a bowl.

6. To make the glaze, add the rest of the spices, soy, honey and salt to the bowl and mix well.

7. Chop the rest of the carrot, onion, celery and garlic and add to a deep roasting dish with 250ml (8fl oz) water.

8. Use a sharp knife to score the gammon fat in a large criss-cross pattern. Place the gammon on top of the vegetables in the roasting dish. Get your little helpers to brush the glaze all over the gammon, ensuring to use all of the mix – this will form the gravy.

9. Roast the gammon in the oven for 1.5-2 hours, ensuring you spoon the glaze over the meat every 15 minutes.

10. While the gammon is cooking, allow the kids to wash the sweet potatoes and then dry using a kitchen towel. Then cut the sweet potato into evenly-sized chunks for roasting, leaving the skin on.

11. Get the little helpers to roll up their sleeves and toss the sweet potato chunks in the olive oil, rosemary, salt and pepper. Line a baking dish with parchment paper and place the coated sweet potato chunks in.

12. 20 minutes before the gammon is fully cooked, put the sweet potatoes into the oven.

13. In the meantime, take the outer leaves of the sprouts off and cook for 3 minutes in a pot of boiling salted water. Strain and leave to cool before cutting the sprouts into quarters. Leave aside for now.

14. Heat some oil in a pan over a medium heat. Once hot, fry the chopped bacon for 2-3 minutes until it becomes crispy. Add in the nutmeg, butter and sprouts, and continue frying until golden in colour.

15. Take the gammon out of the oven and rest for 10 minutes. Cook the roasties for 10 more minutes until crispy.

16. To serve, carve the gammon and plate up along with the roasties and sprouts. Use the leftover juices in the gammon tray as gravy.

FISH AND SEAFOOD RECIPES

Slow Cooker Fire Roasted Tomato Shrimp Tacos

ⓘ Servings: 4-5   ⏱ Cooking Time: 2 Hours

Ingredients:

- 1 pound medium shrimp, peeled and deveined, tails removed (fresh or frozen then thawed) (see notes below for fresh shrimp)
- 1 Tablespoon olive oil (or avocado oil)
- 1 teaspoon minced garlic
- 1/2 cup chopped onion
- 1 bell pepper, chopped (about 1/2 to 2/3 cup)
- 14.5 ounce can fire roasted stewed tomatoes (diced work best)
- 1/2 cup chunky salsa
- kosher salt and black pepper to taste
- 1/2 teaspoon cumin
- 1/2 teaspoon chili powder or ancho chili powder
- 1/4 teaspoon paprika or cayenne pepper
- 2 Tablespoons chopped cilantro (extra for plating)
- Optional toppings – chopped green onion, sour cream, avocado, jalapeño pepper, etc.
- Tortillas to serve (gluten free corn tortillas or grain free low carb tortillas)

Directions:

1. First, prepare the shrimp if they are not already thawed. If using frozen shrimp, quickly thaw in water for 10 minutes before peeling. Pat the shrimp dry with paper towels.
2. Layer the shrimp at the bottom of the crockpot/slow cooker. Drizzle 1 tablespoon olive oil on top. Add the garlic, chopped onion and bell pepper, and toss to combine.
3. Add the drained canned fire roasted tomatoes, salsa, salt, pepper, cumin, chili powder, and paprika to the crockpot. Mix together until seasonings are well combined with shrimp and vegetables.
4. Place slow cooker (crock pot) on low for 2-3 hours or on high for 90 minutes to 2 hours. Stir once, about halfway through cooking.
5. Check on shrimp after about 1 hour of cooking on high. If they look almost done, place on medium for another 30 minutes to an hour.
6. Shrimp are done and cooked through once opaque, looking similar to that of steamed shrimp.
7. Serve with gluten free tortillas and fillings/toppings of choice. Ex: chopped green onions, avocado, jalapeño, and extra cilantro to garnish.
8. These tacos are best enjoyed right away. See notes for storage tips.

Notes:

1. Filling Tips – For thick taco filling be sure to use a chunky salsa with lots of vegetables, not a pureed or restaurant style salsa. If you don't have chili powder, you may use a taco seasoning or other Mexican seasoning of choice. Be sure there are no added gluten-containing ingredients.
2. Storage/Meal Prep Tips – If not serving right away, let the shrimp taco filling cool then store in an airtight container in fridge for up to 3 to 4 days. To reheat, warm taco filling on medium low on stove top or place back in slow cooker on warm setting.

Slow Cooker Poached Salmon

Servings: 4-6

Ingredients:

- 2 cups water
- 1 cup dry white wine
- 1 lemon, thinly sliced
- 1 shallot, thinly sliced
- 1 bay leaf
- 5 to 6 sprigs fresh herbs, such as tarragon, dill, and/or Italian parsley
- 1 teaspoon black peppercorns
- 1 teaspoon kosher salt
- 2 pounds skin-on salmon (or 4-6 fillets), preferably farm-raised
- Kosher salt and freshly ground black pepper
- Lemon wedges, coarse sea salt, and olive oil for serving

Directions:

1. Combine water, wine, lemon, shallots, bay leaf, herbs, peppercorns and salt in the slow cooker and cook on high for 30 minutes.

2. Season the top of the salmon with salt and pepper and place in the slow cooker, skin side down. Cover and cook on low until salmon is opaque in color and flakes gently with a fork. Start checking for desired doneness after 45 minutes to an hour and continue cooking until preferred doneness is reached. (Salmon can be held on the warm setting for several hours.)

3. Drizzle salmon with good-quality olive oil and sprinkle with coarse salt. Serve with lemon wedges on the side.

Smoked Salmon & Lemon Risotto

Servings: 4   **Cooking Time: 20 Mins.**

Ingredients:

- 1 onion, finely chopped
- 2 tbsp olive oil
- 350g risotto rice, such as Arborio
- 1 garlic clove, finely chopped
- 1 ½l boiling vegetable stock
- 170g pack smoked salmon, three-quarters chopped
- 85g mascarpone lite
- 3 tbsp flat-leaf parsley, chopped
- grated lemon zest, plus squeeze of juice
- handful rocket

Directions:

1. Fry the onion in the oil for 5 mins. Add the rice and garlic, then cook for 2 mins, stirring continuously. Pour in a third of the stock and set the timer to 20 mins. Simmer, stirring occasionally, until the stock has been absorbed, then add half the rest of the stock and carry on cooking, stirring a bit more frequently, until that has been absorbed.

2. Pour in the last of the stock, stir, then simmer until cooked and creamy. Take from the heat and add the chopped salmon, mascarpone, parsley and lemon zest. Grind in some black pepper, but don't add salt as the salmon will be salty enough. Leave for 5 mins to settle, then taste and add a little lemon juice if you like. Serve topped with reserved salmon (roughly torn) and some rocket.

Slow-roasted Blue-eye With Tomatoes And Olives

Servings: 8

Ingredients:

- 3 x 400g skinless blue-eye fillets
- 500g mixed baby heirloom tomatoes
- 1/3 cup (40g) pitted black olives
- 1/3 cup (55g) caperberries, rinsed, drained
- 1 bunch flat-leaf parsley, leaves chopped, stalks reserved
- 100ml dry white wine
- 1/3 cup (80ml) extra virgin olive oil
- Crusty bread, to serve

Directions:

1. Preheat the oven to 150°C and line a baking dish with baking paper.
2. Place the fish in prepared dish and season with salt. Cut the larger tomatoes in half and keep the smaller ones whole.
3. Scatter on top and around fish with olives, caperberries and reserved parsley stalks.
4. Drizzle over wine and oil, then cover dish with foil and bake for 30-35 minutes until fish is almost cooked through.
5. Transfer fish to a serving plate and cover with foil (residual heat will continue cooking fish).
6. Increase the oven to 180°C and cook the tomato mixture for a further 15-20 minutes until starting to collapse.
7. Scatter tomato mixture over fish with parsley leaves. Serve with crusty bread.

DESSERT RECIPES

Slow Cooker Apple Butter Recipe

 Servings: 12   Cooking Time: 10 Hours

Ingredients:

- 3 pounds Granny Smith apples
- 2 (3-pound/50-ounce) jars unsweetened applesauce
- 4 cups sugar
- 1 1/2 cups apple juice
- 2 teaspoons ground cinnamon
- 1teaspoon ground cloves
- 1 teaspoon ground allspice

Directions:

1. Peel, core and cut the apples into small chips. Put all the ingredients into a slow cooker and stir. Cover and cook on low overnight, about 8 to 10 hours. Remove the cover, stir and taste. Add more spices or sugar, if desired. Continue cooking for a few more hours, uncovered, until some of the liquid is reduced and the butter has cooked down a bit. Pour into sterilized jars and refrigerate.

2. Serve over hot biscuits, toast, scones, or just eat it out of the jar if no one is looking!

Choc Chip Banana Cake

 Servings: 8   Cooking Time: 40 Mins.

Ingredients:

- 3 bananas mashed ripe
- 2 tbs butter
- 3/4 cup sugar
- 1 egg
- 1 1/2 cups self-raising flour
- 1 tsp bicarbonate of soda
- 2 tbs milk
- 3/4 cup chocolate chips

Directions:

1. Preheat oven to 180C.
2. Cream butter and sugar together.
3. Add the remaining Ingredients and beat well.
4. Pour mixture into a greased doughnut tin or 2 greased long tins.
5. Bake for 35-40 minutes.

Slow-cooker Jar Cakes

Servings: 8   **Cooking Time: 3 Hours 5 Mins.**

Ingredients:

- 250g frozen mixed berries
- 1/4 cup (55g) caster sugar
- 125g butter, softened
- 1 cup (220g) caster sugar, extra
- 3 Coles Australian Free Range Eggs
- 1/2 cup (40g) desiccated coconut
- 1/2 cup (75g) plain flour
- 1/4 cup (40g) self-raising flour
- 1/3 cup (95g) vanilla yoghurt
- Pink liquid food colouring
- Mixed berries, to decorate
- Coconut frosting
- 100g butter, softened
- 500g icing sugar mixture
- 1/4 cup (60ml) coconut milk

Directions:

1. Combine berries and sugar in a large saucepan over medium heat. Cook, stirring occasionally, for 5 mins or until berries release their juices and mixture thickens slightly. Set aside to cool.

2. Use an electric mixer to beat butter and extra sugar in a bowl until pale and creamy. Add eggs, 1 at a time, beating well after each addition. Add the coconut and combined flour and stir to combine. Stir in the yoghurt.

3. Spoon berry mixture evenly among eight 1-cup (250ml) jars. Top with one-third of the cake mixture. Tint the remaining cake mixture pink with food colouring. Spoon half the mixture evenly among the jars. Smooth surface. Tint remaining cake mixture a more intense pink with more food colouring. Divide evenly among jars and smooth surface (jars should only be about one-third to half full). Place lids loosely over jars.

4. Place half the jars in a slow cooker. Pour boiling water into the slow cooker to come 4cm up the side of the jars. Cover and cook for 1 1/2 hours on high or until a skewer inserted into the centres comes out clean. Set aside to cool. Repeat with the remaining jars.

5. To make the coconut frosting, use an electric mixer to beat the butter in a bowl until very pale. Add icing sugar, in batches, beating well after each addition. Beat in coconut milk. Place in a piping bag fitted with a 1cm fluted nozzle. Pipe frosting onto the cakes. Top with berries.

Slow-cooked Mac 'n' Cheese

 Servings: 9   Cooking Time: 2-1/2 Hours

Ingredients:

- 2 cups uncooked elbow macaroni
- 1 can (12 ounces) evaporated milk
- 1-1/2 cups whole milk
- 2 large eggs
- 1/4 cup butter, melted
- 1 teaspoon salt
- 2-1/2 cups shredded cheddar cheese
- 2-1/2 cups shredded sharp cheddar cheese, divided

Directions:

1. Cook macaroni according to package directions; drain and rinse in cold water. In a large bowl, combine the evaporated milk, whole milk, eggs, butter and salt. Stir in the cheddar cheese, 2 cups sharp cheddar cheese and macaroni.
2. Transfer to a greased 3-qt. slow cooker. Cover and cook on low for 2-1/2 to 3 hours or until center is set, stirring once. Sprinkle with remaining sharp cheddar cheese.

Blueberry Cobbler

 Servings: 6   Cooking Time: 3 Hours

Ingredients:

- 1 can (21 ounces) blueberry pie filling
- 1 package (9 ounces) yellow cake mix
- 1/4 cup chopped pecans
- 1/4 cup butter, melted
- Vanilla ice cream, optional

Directions:

1. Place pie filling in a greased 1-1/2-qt. slow cooker. Sprinkle with cake mix and pecans. Drizzle with butter. Cover and cook on high for 3 hours or until topping is golden brown. Serve warm, with ice cream if desired.

Slow-cooker Sticky Date Pudding

👪 Servings: 8   🕐 Cooking Time: 1 Hours 50 Mins.

Ingredients:

- 1 1/4 cups self-raising flour
- 1 1/2 cups brown sugar
- 2/3 cup milk
- 1 egg
- 50g butter, melted, plus 25g extra chopped
- 1 tsp vanilla bean paste
- 200g fresh dates, pitted, finely chopped
- 2 cups boiling water
- Double cream, to serve

Directions:

1. Spray inside of slow-cooker bowl.
2. Combine flour and 1/2 cup sugar in a large bowl. Whisk milk, egg, butter and vanilla in a jug until combined. Pour over flour mixture and stir until smooth. Stir through dates. Pour into prepared slow-cooker bowl.
3. Sprinkle with remaining sugar. Dot with extra butter. Gently pour over boiling water. Cook, covered, on high for 1 hour 40 minutes or until a crust forms and top springs back when pressed with finger.
4. Turn off slow-cooker. Stand pudding, uncovered, in bowl for 10 minutes. Serve with cream.

Peanut Choc Chip Biscuits

Servings: 40   Cooking Time: 15 Mins.

Ingredients:

- 125 g butter
- 1/4 cup peanut butter
- 1 cup brown sugar
- 1/2 cup unsalted roasted peanuts roughly chopped
- 1 egg
- 3/4 cup self-raising flour
- 3/4 cup plain flour
- 1/2 cup rolled oats
- 1 cup milk chocolate chips

Directions:

1. Melt butter and peanut butter together, allow to cool.
2. Combine brown sugar and egg with butter mixture, then add flours, peanuts, oats and chocolate chips.
3. Mix well.
4. Roll into walnut-sized balls and flatten with a fork.
5. Bake at 180C for 12-14 minutes.

Notes:

1. Biscuits don't spread during cooking so make sure they are well flattened.
2. For a change, add a few sultanas, peanuts and crushed cornflakes to the mixture.

Best Ever Chocolate Brownies Recipe

Servings: 16   **Cooking Time: 27-35 Mins.**

Ingredients:

- 185g unsalted butter
- 185g best dark chocolate
- 85g plain flour
- 40g cocoa powder
- 50g white chocolate
- 50g milk chocolate
- 3 large eggs
- 275g golden caster sugar

Directions:

1. Cut 185g unsalted butter into small cubes and tip into a medium bowl. Break 185g dark chocolate into small pieces and drop into the bowl.

2. Fill a small saucepan about a quarter full with hot water, then sit the bowl on top so it rests on the rim of the pan, not touching the water. Put over a low heat until the butter and chocolate have melted, stirring occasionally to mix them.

3. Remove the bowl from the pan. Alternatively, cover the bowl loosely with cling film and put in the microwave for 2 minutes on High. Leave the melted mixture to cool to room temperature.

4. While you wait for the chocolate to cool, position a shelf in the middle of your oven and turn the oven on to 180C/160C fan/gas

5. Using a shallow 20cm square tin, cut out a square of kitchen foil (or non-stick baking parchment) to line the base. Tip 85g plain flour and 40g cocoa powder into a sieve held over a medium bowl. Tap and shake the sieve so they run through together and you get rid of any lumps.

6. Chop 50g white chocolate and 50g milk chocolate into chunks on a board.

7. Break 3 large eggs into a large bowl and tip in 275g golden caster sugar. With an electric mixer on maximum speed, whisk the eggs and sugar. They will look thick and creamy, like a milk shake. This can take 3-8 minutes, depending on how powerful your mixer is. You'll know it's ready when the mixture becomes really pale and about double its original volume. Another check is to turn off the mixer, lift out the beaters and wiggle them from side to side. If the mixture that runs off the beaters leaves a trail on the surface of the mixture in the bowl for a second or two, you're there.

8. Pour the cooled chocolate mixture over the eggy mousse, then gently fold together with a rubber spatula. Plunge the spatula in at one side, take it underneath and bring it up the opposite side and in again at the middle. Continue going under and over in a figure of eight, moving the bowl round after each folding so you can get at it from all sides, until the two mixtures are one and the colour is a mottled dark brown. The idea is to marry them without knocking out the air, so be as gentle and slow as you like.

9. Hold the sieve over the bowl of eggy chocolate mixture and resift the cocoa and flour mixture, shaking the sieve from side to side, to cover the top evenly.

10. Gently fold in this powder using the same figure of eight action as before. The mixture will look dry and dusty at first, and a bit unpromising, but if you keep going very gently brand patiently, it will end up looking gungy and

fudgy. Stop just before you feel you should, as you don't want to overdo this mixing.

11. Finally, stir in the white and milk chocolate chunks until they're dotted throughout.

12. Pour the mixture into the prepared tin, scraping every bit out of the bowl with the spatula. Gently ease the mixture into the corners of the tin and paddle the spatula from side to side across the top to level it.

13. Put in the oven and set your timer for 25 mins. When the buzzer goes, open the oven, pull the shelf out a bit and gently shake the tin. If the brownie wobbles in the middle, it's not quite done, so slide it back in and bake for another 5 minutes until the top has a shiny, papery crust and the sides are just beginning to come away from the tin. Take out of the oven.

14. Leave the whole thing in the tin until completely cold, then, if you're using the brownie tin, lift up the protruding rim slightly and slide the uncut brownie out on its base. If you're using a normal tin, lift out the brownie with the foil (or parchment). Cut into quarters, then cut each quarter into four squares and finally into triangles.

15. They'll keep in an airtight container for a good two weeks and in the freezer for up to a month.

Easy Chocolate Chip Slice

👥 Servings: 6   🕐 Cooking Time: 35 Mins.

Ingredients:

- 1 cup self-raising flour
- 1 cup coconut
- 3/4 cup caster sugar
- 3/4 cup milk
- 3/4 cup choc chips

Directions:

1. Line a 19cm x 29cm lamington pan with baking paper.

2. Combine all Ingredients in a large bowl and mix well.

3. Spread mixture into prepared pan.

4. Bake at 180C for approximately 35 minutes, or until cooked when tested with a skewer.

5. Allow to cool for 10 minutes before turning out onto a wire rack.

6. Cool completely before cutting into squares.

7. NOTES

8. Because this slice can be frozen, I usually make a double batch, and have found that I only need to add 1¼ cups of both sugar and choc bits, but double all other quantities.

Slow-roasted Rhubarb With Ginger Ice Cream

Servings: 6   **Cooking Time: 1 Hours 25 Mins.**

Ingredients:

- 800g best-quality rhubarb, sliced into thumb-size chunks
- 100ml dessert wine (optional)
- 300g caster sugar
- 2 oranges, zest removed in large strips
- For the ice cream
- 200g stem ginger, very finely chopped, plus a few tsp of syrup
- 250ml full-fat milk
- 4 egg yolks
- 85g caster sugar
- 300ml double cream
- shortbread rounds (optional), to serve

Directions:

1. Make the ice cream: tip the ginger and syrup into a pan with the milk, bring to the boil, then remove from the heat. Allow to cool and infuse, then taste – add more ginger if you like a stronger flavour.

2. Bring the milk and ginger back to the boil. In a separate bowl, mix the yolks with sugar. Pour on the boiled milk, stirring non-stop, until completely mixed, then pour back into the pan. Cook over a gentle heat, stirring constantly, until it thickens and coats the spoon. Remove from the heat and stir in the cream. Pour through a sieve to remove the ginger, cool, then churn in an ice-cream maker. Freeze.

3. Tip the rhubarb into a baking dish, pour over the wine (if using) and scatter over the sugar and zest. Cover with baking paper and bake in a low oven at 140C/ 120C fan/gas 1 for 1 hr or until tender. This slow Directions: keeps the rhubarb's shape and texture. Can be prepared the day ahead and left at room temperature. Serve the rhubarb and its juices along with a couple of scoops of ice cream.

Printed in Great Britain
by Amazon

32159174R00064